CLARK'S

BIG

BOOK OF
BARGAINS

ALSO BY

CLARK HOWARD + MARK MELTZER

Get Clark Smart

CLARK'S BIG BOOK OF BARGAINS

CLARK HOWARD + MARK MELTZER

 HYPERION   NEW YORK

ISBN: 0-7868-8778-8

Hyperion books are available for special promotions and premiums. For details contact Hyperion Special Markets, 77 West 66th Street, 11th floor, New York, New York 10023, or call 212-456-0133.

FIRST EDITION

10 9 8 7 6 5 4 3 2 1

For Rebecca, Stephanie, Nicholas, and Courtney.
As they grow, may they learn to spend
less than they earn.

And to Lane and Nancy for their continued
love and support.

CONTENTS

ACKNOWLEDGMENTS

A lot of people deserve thanks for helping this book become a reality. Foremost amongst them are my agent, Laurie Liss of Sterling Lord Literistic, and my editor, Mary Ellen O'Neill of Hyperion Books. *Clark's Big Book of Bargains* would not exist without their efforts. Special thanks also goes to Christa DiBiase, executive producer of my radio show and chief researcher for this book, and to Nancy Meltzer, wife of my co-author, Mark Meltzer, whose ideas can be found in many of the chapters.

In the course of writing this, I often ran into areas where I needed expert help, and a lot of people gave generously of their time, ideas, and knowledge to help. They include the following:

Mary Abreu   Dr. J. Crystal Baxter   Joshua Bowden

Brian Butler   Lisa Carlson   Kim Curley   Kimberly Drobes

Karen Gerson Duncan   Dain Ferrero   Judith Greenberg

Jerry Hennon   Dr. Thomas C. Jagor   Dr. Bob Kim   Mark Kenady

Daniel Kolber   Jim Molis   Dr. Nicholas W. Petty

Greg Turchetta

A NOTE FROM CLARK

This book is about spending money, something we do every day, but sometimes without a lot of thought. We spend our money in so many ways, large and small, that sometimes we wonder where our paycheck went. I'd like every dollar you earn to buy more and last longer.

One of the reasons I wrote *Clark's Big Book of Bargains* is to show you how to treasure hunt, how to have fun—as I do—finding great deals. For example, I'll show you how to buy a box of disposable contact lenses for $13.95, a bouquet of roses on Valentine's Day for $19, and a great bottle of wine for less than $8.

I also want to share my philosophy of spending and give you a new way to think about the choices you make each time you open your wallet. Instead of burning your paycheck, nurse it, so you can get more of the things you want in life.

Making better spending decisions lets you take control of your life and gain more financial security. Every day on my radio show, I talk to listeners around the country whose spending, and the resulting debt, is causing tremendous stress in their lives. Is it worth having the possessions you have, if underneath it all, you're trying to figure out how to pay the bills? I want to help you turn down the pressure, so you don't have to worry when you open the mailbox about the bills waiting for you.

The average American now owes more money than they earn in a year, according to data compiled by the *Wall Street Journal*. Never in history has that happened, and it's deeply disturbing. Just ten years ago, we carried far less debt than we do today. And this isn't just a problem for lower-income or middle-class people. High-income families, those in the top fifth of U.S. households, are carrying debt averaging 20 percent more than their disposable income, according to the *Wall Street Journal*. If you get anything out of this book, I hope it will be the idea that this is a choice people have made, not a necessity.

The answer is simple. It's not what you earn that matters—it's what you spend. If you spend less than you earn, you can take the dollars you don't consume, and put them aside to build long-term financial security for you, your children, their education, and your retirement.

This book is about choices you can make that will allow you to live a debt-free lifestyle, or at the very least, a lifestyle that puts you in control of your finances.

Some of the things you'll read in here might sound a little strange, like feeding your baby generic formula, or buying used furniture. I'm certainly not suggesting you do everything you read here. This isn't like a recipe, where you have to follow the steps carefully, and only then will the dish taste good. Look for ideas that work for you, and add your own. You may have ideas that are better than what I suggest. The goal is to create a new way of thinking about spending, before you spend. Perhaps you've always gone to a major oil company station to buy gasoline, you have that company's credit card, and you go there without thinking. Instead, think about going to a discount gas station. Just making that one change will put a few extra dollars in your pocket every week. Or let's say you normally buy Tide detergent at the supermarket. What if instead you bought Tide at a discount store, or if you bought the store-brand detergent and tried it? Maybe you'll like it and use it again and again.

I hope *Clark's Big Book of Bargains* helps you get more for your money and feel better about your financial future.

Clark Howard

CLARK'S BIG BOOK OF BARGAINS

CHAPTER 1

FOOD

We all have different approaches to food. My goal is to enjoy it. Yours may be to eat all the right things. But however you look at food, I want you to buy it at the right price.

I have lots of money-saving tips for you to reduce your food budget, whether you eat at home, eat out, or bring home ready-to-eat meals. As to what you drink, alcoholic or non-alcoholic, there are tremendous savings available in that area as well.

In this chapter, I'll show you how to save at the grocery store and at the restaurant, whether it's white tablecloth, middle-market, or fast food. And I'll show you how to save on a bottle of wine or a bottle of water to go with your meal.

I expect people to have the strongest reaction to this chapter of any in this book. I hope you'll share with me your favorite ways to save on food and beverages. Maybe we can include them in a future edition.

One of the few places virtually everyone spends money is the supermarket, and it's a prime place to save.

There are a few common-sense rules that can help you save on your grocery bill. You may be using one or more occasionally already, but you probably don't follow them consistently.

The first is to shop with a list. If you go into a supermarket without a list, you're going to fall prey to the store's marketing tactics. You'll buy things that are displayed at "end caps," at the end of each aisle. You'll be tempted by merchandise that is positioned at eye level, often foods with a lot of fat and calories that will earn a higher profit for the store and also be bad for your health. The store's goal is to get you to buy things you hadn't intended to buy. Using a list helps you fight that.

My wife, Lane, is obsessive about lists. She figures out exactly what she needs, goes down the aisles, and picks out only those items.

The second rule is never go to the supermarket when you're hungry. That is a fatal error for your finances, because you're much more likely to make impulse buys when you're hungry. If you do just those two things, you can make an enormous difference in your grocery bill.

There are a number of techniques that will help you save money on the things you buy. One is using discount coupons. I judged a newspaper contest on handling money, and it was tough to pick a winner, because each of the contestants had brilliant strategies. One woman took $500 and turned it into $1,900 worth of food, simply by couponing. It was phenomenal. She did her shopping at four different stores, and was very organized about it. She went through the fliers each week to see what they were offering. If a store doubled or tripled coupons on certain days, she would shop there on those days. That may make your eyes roll, because that's a lot of work and a lot of time. But if you can take $500 and turn it into $1,900 by spending a little time organizing yourself and going to four stores, that seems well worth the effort. Normally, you're not going to spend $500 on groceries at one time, but I love the idea of being able to get double or triple the value for your money simply by buying items that are on sale or couponable.

There are a couple of dangers to coupons. One is that you'll buy products you don't need, just because you have a coupon. Or you'll fall victim to the manufacturer's strategy, which is to get you hooked on a product with a coupon, so you'll buy it again and again at full price. The woman who nearly quadrupled her money using coupons doesn't get tricked into making impulse purchases and she isn't brand loyal, so she'll freely switch brands depending on what coupons she has. She's loyal to saving money, not to the brand.

There are a number of Web sites you can go to to get grocery coupons. Among them are www.cutouthunger. org, salesmountain.com, and coupon mountain.com.

A number of supermarkets and phar-macies across the country, including CVS, Kroger, Harris Teeter, and Price-Chopper, are now offering discount cards that customers use to obtain advertised special prices. You don't pay anything for the cards. You simply show them at the register upon checkout to receive the special discounts. Many people don't like them because the store can track your purchases with the card, and people believe this is an invasion of privacy. I'm willing to give up some of my privacy in exchange for bargain prices, but you might want to avoid using the card when you are making a purchase you wouldn't want tracked (for example, some type of medication you feel is private).

Another savings strategy is to shop the warehouse clubs, like Sam's Club, Costco, and BJ's, which have had an enormous impact on the grocery business. If you want to save on your grocery bill and you can work with a more limited selection, you should buy at least some of your groceries at a warehouse club. Roughly a third of the merchandise in the warehouse clubs are grocery-type items, and their prices are significantly lower than the regular prices at the grocery store; however, they probably will not be lower than the *sale* prices at the grocery store. When Lane goes to Costco or Sam's, she's not able to get everything she wants. So she goes there about once a month, and does the rest of the grocery shopping at regular supermarkets. She buys all the paper goods and the non-perishables at the warehouse club and then picks up the perishables at the supermarket, along with the brand-name products she wants but can't get at the warehouse club.

If you're not a regular warehouse club shopper, you may think all you're going to get there is a restaurant-size jar of mayonnaise. But it's not like that anymore. They may make you buy two of a regular-size item—two supermarket-size bottles of apple juice, for example. But you don't have to buy giant-size packages, like on an old *Seinfeld* episode.

Be careful about product sizes at your regular supermarket. The larger sizes of products used to give you the best value. But not anymore. Manufacturers figured out that people who buy the extra-large size just want more of it. They're not necessarily looking to save money. So you'll typically pay more per ounce—not less—by buying the extra-large size of an item rather than the regular size. That's especially true of convenience foods. Take a $5 pocket calculator with you when you go to the supermarket, in case the store doesn't have shelf tags with the unit prices. I know it seems tedious, but you can quickly divide the price per number of items and get a unit price, to see which size is the best deal.

If a product that you buy regularly is on sale, make sure to stock up. If your favorite soda is 89 cents for a 2-liter bottle, buy five or ten bottles. Then you won't have to buy it when the price goes up to $1.29 a bottle. That's a slam dunk.

Another way to save is to shop at one of the two discounters that are changing the supermarket business: Wal-Mart, which is well on its way to becoming the nation's largest supermarket chain, and Aldi, a deep-discount chain that is spreading across the country. Wal-Mart's supercenters, which are combination Wal-Mart stores and grocery stores, almost without question have the lowest grocery prices, because groceries aren't as important to the company as getting people to buy items on both sides of the store.

Aldi uses a smaller store format, and while it sells both perishables and non-perishables, it limits the selection to a tiny fraction of what's available in a normal supermarket. By doing that, it's able to sell merchandise at a much higher volume, with lower prices. I visited an Aldi store recently and I was amazed at how low the prices were, compared to my regular supermarket. Milk was $1 cheaper per gallon. Bread was just 39 cents a loaf. Aldi sells a few brand names, but focuses on its store brands. And customers I talked with said they love the quality of Aldi's store brands.

I went to an Aldi store a few minutes before 9 A.M., and people were lined up outside waiting to get in. The parking lot was full. I was floored.

Aldi shoppers said they estimate they could buy $100 worth of groceries at Aldi for $55 to $60. I saw a study that said grocery shopping at the big supermarket chains Kroger and Albertson's costs shoppers 38 percent to 43 percent more than buying groceries at Wal-Mart.

You can save a lot of money by trying store-brand products, which, though more profitable for the supermarket, are usually cheaper, and the quality of store brands is very good in most categories. Here's what I'd like you to do: Try the store-brand food, and if you don't like it in a particular category, don't buy it anymore and go back to the brand name. You've wasted your money one time on something that tasted lousy. But if you find a store brand you like, you're going to save money every time you go to the store. That will save you more money than shopping in a warehouse club, buying with coupons, or any other method.

The price difference between name-brand and store-brand products is remarkable. Costco's brand of facial tissue is 53 cents per 100 sheets. Kleenex brand is more than $1 per 100 sheets, even at Costco. So it's double the money for the brand name. It may turn out the store brand of tissue or paper towel isn't soft enough or strong enough and you don't like it. So you don't buy it again.

Don't buy non-food items in a supermarket, period. In the non-food aisles, supermarkets are selling convenience, not economy. If you buy your toilet paper, soaps, detergents, or diapers for your kids in a supermarket, you'll be eating up your wallet. That's why Wal-Mart scares the daylights out of major supermarkets, because those have been massive profit categories for the supermarkets. Wal-Mart sells its groceries at a lower markup and it sells the non-groceries at a lower markup. Batteries are a good example. If you buy them at a supermarket, you should have your car keys taken away from you, because the markup on an item like that at a su-

permarket is astronomical. Buy them at a discount store, and buy generic alkaline batteries, which are just as good as the top brands and much cheaper. Costco, for example, had a box of forty-eight store-brand alkaline double-A batteries for about $10.50. The brand-name batteries were about $11.50 for twenty-four batteries. Buy them at a supermarket and you'll probably pay $10 for eight batteries. You have to decide if you're going to a supermarket for convenience or to save money, because they're completely different things.

Supermarkets also charge more for convenience foods, but not always, and even if they do, that isn't always bad. Something that's cooked for you or chopped up for you may cost more than something you had to prepare yourself. But it may not. *Consumer Reports* studied prepackaged bags of salad greens, expecting to find it was a terrible rip-off compared to the cost of buying lettuce and carrots and chopping them up yourself. But the magazine found the salad bags were fairly priced.

It's still far less expensive to buy a prepared meal in a supermarket than it is to pay for a meal in a restaurant. In 1999, the average family spent $2,116, or $846 a person, on meals away from home, according to the National Restaurant Association. Eating at restaurants accounted for more than 42 percent of their food dollars. Higher-income families, those earning $70,000 or more, spend more than half their food dollars in restaurants.

So many families today are very time-pressed and won't cook. It's easier to eat out than to buy the ingredients and make the chili from scratch, but keep in mind, you can spend a *lot* of money this way.

The same goes for take-out meals that are meant to replace a home-cooked dinner. Figure out the cost per person for the meal to see if it's an economical choice. If a take-out chicken dinner for four costs $20, that's $5 a person, which is pretty good. Or you might buy a pre-roasted chicken and make a side dish and a vegetable at home. It can be an affordable alternative to a home-cooked or restaurant meal.

So what should your game plan be for slicing your grocery bill? That's up to you. There is no one strategy that will get it done. Try one of the things I've suggested, and see what you're comfortable with. Formulate a plan and use it consistently. Your goal should be to get away from buying on a haphazard basis, with no thought or planning.

• Tips on Supermarkets •

○ Shop with a list, and never go shopping when you're hungry.

○ Try using discount coupons, especially when stores double or triple their value. But don't buy things you don't need, or get locked in to specific brands.

- ❍ Buy at least some of your groceries at warehouse clubs, which have lower prices but less variety of merchandise.

- ❍ Shop at discount grocers such as Wal-Mart and Aldi.

- ❍ Try store brands. The quality is very good and prices usually are much lower.

- ❍ Don't buy non-food items, such as paper towels or batteries, at a traditional supermarket.

- ❍ Don't worry about paying more for prepared foods at a supermarket if they keep you from buying a more expensive meal at a restaurant.

• Internet •

www.cutouthunger.org
www.salesmountain.com
www.couponmountain.com

✳ RESTAURANTS ✳

I'm a frequent violator of the first rule of saving money on food, which is *Eat at home.* I eat about 80 percent of my meals out, and that's not a smart financial strategy. But if you do want to eat out—at least occasionally—and not spend a fortune, I have some tips that will make an enormous difference in what you spend.

In a fine restaurant, the big profit centers for the restaurant are alcohol, appetizers, and dessert. You'll lower the bill by about a third if you treat the main course as the main reason you've gone out, and avoid all the extras, especially the alcohol and the dessert. If you like to have a drink before your meal, have a glass of wine before you go to the restaurant. You have to know yourself. If one drink would impair your driving, don't have it.

I get a lot of heat from people on this idea, because they say part of going out to a nice restaurant is to throw caution to the winds and not worry about price. And that may be fine, especially for a special event like a birthday or an anniversary. But I look at restaurants the way I do travel. If you travel economically, you create more opportunity to travel. If you eat out economically, you're free to eat out more frequently. Instead of treating a restaurant meal as a very rare, extra-special pleasure, where you spend a fortune whenever you go, why not instead afford yourself the opportunity to enjoy that special experience more often? It just takes some discipline. Think about it. You'd normally pay as much for a glass of wine in a nice restaurant as a whole bottle that you would drink at home. The cost of a mixed drink to a restaurant usually is around 25 cents—for a drink that will cost you $4 to $6. It's an enormously expensive markup.

If you enjoy wine with your dinner, you might be able to bring your own, depending on the law where you live. If it's legal, many different kinds of restaurants will allow this, even very upscale ones. Call ahead and ask, and tell the restaurant, "We have our own favorite wine." Then you don't sound so nervy. If they allow it, they'll charge a "corkage" fee, usually $3 to $10 for each bottle, which covers their cost to uncork the wine and serve it, using their glasses. The markup on a bottle of wine is so large that you'll still save a lot of money. I'm told that the truly classy thing to do is bring a nice bottle of wine that the restaurant doesn't serve. If it's really nice, you can offer the maitre d' a taste.

Desserts take an even bigger bite out of your wallet than alcohol. They're gigantically profitable for the restaurant—that's why they make such a show of presenting the dessert tray. My wife, Lane, had a dessert recently that she just adores. It's a sliver of waffle, two microscopic scoops of ice cream, some caramel and some fudge—and would you believe, it was $9! The cost of the ingredients couldn't have hit 50 cents. Desserts are the Bermuda Triangle for your money.

Another thing to beware of are the "specials." Some people feel it's impolite to ask the cost when a server is describing the specials, but to me it's impolite that the description doesn't include the cost. I ask. One of my radio show staffers, Joni Alpert, ordered a lobster special one night, and later was shocked to find that her dinner cost $72. Joni was so embarrassed. She and her husband, Hal, were out with friends, and she never would have ordered the lobster if she knew how expensive it was. Restaurants often use the specials to get an extra-large profit out of you.

At mid-level restaurants, the best way to save money is the time of day you visit. While high-end restaurants would not stoop so low as to have peak and off-peak pricing, mid-priced restaurants are very practical about this. They'll offer early-bird or late-evening savings opportunities, or a limited menu of special items if you order before 7 P.M. Let the clock work for you. If the restaurant managers know it's going to be packed at 7 P.M., and you're willing to help them with their traffic flow by eating a bargain at 6 P.M., do it. Early-bird specials always were a joke about elderly people in Arizona and Florida, but the way I look at it, the joke's on me if I don't take advantage of it.

One of the coolest ways to save money at high-end restaurants is to eat lunch there instead of dinner. The lunch menu usually will have the same or similar items as the dinner menu, but they're cheaper at lunch because there's price resistance to what people will pay before dark. So you can have the same elegant level of food and service for half the price, or less. You'll get a slightly smaller portion, but not equivalent to the difference in price. That tells you what kind of markup there is on food at a high-end restaurant.

So many restaurants now give portions that are ridiculously large. They're just too big to eat. You can either try to eat it all and end up stuffed, or take it home and, as so many people do, throw it away. So why not split an entree with someone, if you both like the same item, even if you have to pay a plate charge? My co-author, Mark Meltzer, likes to take the leftovers to work for lunch the next day, and heats them up in the microwave. He does that with home-cooked dinners also, and as a result he eats well and spends very little each month eating lunch out. But most restaurant leftovers, while taken home with good intentions, end up in the trash.

Since I don't buy a lot of extras at restaurants, I have a lower total bill, and that could mean short-changing the server. So if the server has been delight-ful, I often tip 25 percent of the bill, much more than the 15 to 20 percent guideline. I may be frugal, but I believe in being generous when it comes to tipping.

If you want to learn more about the restaurants in a city you may be planning to visit, try picking up a copy of the local city magazine, or reading the food column online from the local newspaper. There's also the *Zagat Survey*, which is available online (www.zagat.com) for a subscription fee. These sources may help steer you to restaurants that offer better value.

• Tips on Restaurants •

- ❍ At a fine restaurant, you'll chop a third off your bill if you avoid alcohol, appetizers, and desserts.

- ❍ Ask the price of the "special" before you order. Restaurants like to get extra-large profits out of these choices.

- ❍ Visit a fine restaurant for lunch instead of dinner. You'll get the same food for much less money.

- ❍ At mid-level restaurants, take advantage of off-peak prices, such as early-bird and late-night discounts.

❍ If the restaurant gives giant-size portions, try sharing an entree with a companion.

• Internet •

www.zagat.com

✳ FAST FOOD ✳

In a high-end restaurant, buying the "special" can cost you. But at fast-food restaurants, where I have my greatest culinary expertise, buying the special will save you a lot of money.

Most fast-food restaurants offer rotating specials featuring one of their burgers or sandwiches. For example, McDonald's has a chicken sandwich and a fish sandwich, each currently on sale for 99 cents, and Burger King has a number of items on its 99-cent menu. Wendy's has a regular 99-cent menu, but it's the only one of the fast-food restaurants that does it that way.

You'll do your body and your wallet a favor if you buy whatever burger or sandwich is on special and skip the french fries, which are the highest profit-margin

item. Your doctor would be happy to tell you that french fries aren't his or her choice for you as a vegetable anyway.

Fast-food restaurants love to sell you "combo" meals, and tell you what a great discount you're getting by buying them, because the burger, fries, and drink cost less in the combo than they would if you bought them individually.

Wendy's is an interesting example, because it does something you're not supposed to do, and that's price for two different customers in the same restaurant. Wendy's has the ultra-large burger, fries, and drink combo at a very high price, usually $5 to $6, and also appeals to the price-oriented shopper with a 99-cent menu line. Can you guess which of the menu boards I order from? It's become almost a cliché about me that I do some burger rearranging when I go to Wendy's. I buy two 99-cent "double-stacks" with cheese and put them together, giving me a half-pound cheese-burger for $1.98. That's the same amount of burger I'd get if I bought Wendy's half-pounder with cheese, which is more than a dollar more. (I could eat the double-stacks separately, but then I'd have too much bread.) It's just using their menu to my advantage.

Drinks are pretty expensive too, even at 99 cents. My co-author, Mark Meltzer, often buys a burger and a salad at Wendy's for $1.98, and takes it back to the office to enjoy with a 50-cent drink from the vending machine, a glass of water, or a soda he brought from home and chilled in the office refrigerator. You may think I'm crazy, watching a few dollars to this degree, but it adds up. According to an article in the April 2000 issue of *Money* magazine, if you skip the $4 gourmet coffee and croissant every morning and instead put the $80 a month into a mutual fund, you could have $146,000 in twenty-five years (assuming a 12 per-cent annualized market return). Saving a few dollars a day on breakfast or lunch can turn into a lot of money.

Another way to save is to look for coupons for fast-food restaurants. Mark bought a coupon-filled calendar at Chick-fil-A for $5, got a free chicken salad sandwich immediately, and throughout the year got several free or almost-free lunches. He saved probably $20 to $30 for the $5 he spent on the calendar.

The venerable "Entertainment" coupon book is especially good for saving money on mid-priced and fast-food restaurants, with a lot of buy-one, get-one-free offers. If you use one of these books, you'll get a tremendous payback. But you have to keep it with you in your car. The purpose of these deals is to get you into a place that maybe you don't visit enough, or to introduce a new restaurant to you that you wouldn't have used otherwise. But even if you use it only for restaurants you like to frequent, you'll get a nice payback. Look through one first though, to make sure it has places you might like. The coupon books are not cheap—$8 to $25 depending on the city and the seller.

• Tips on Fast Food •

○ Skip the fries and buy the sandwich that's on special.

○ Don't buy the "combo" meals.

○ Look for discount coupons, either the free kind or coupons you can buy in coupon books.

• Internet •

www.entertainment.com

✳ LEARNING TO COOK ✳

One of the easiest ways to save money on food is to eat at home more and eat out less. But a lot of twenty- and thirty-something people don't know how to cook well enough to eat at home. As a result, people under age twenty-five spend 45.5 percent of their food dollars eating out, a higher percentage than any other age category, according to the National Restaurant Association. The twenty-five-to thirty-four-year-olds aren't far behind, spending 43.8 percent of their food budget to dine out.

The lack of expertise of Generation Xers and Generation Yers in the kitchen has prompted a new wave of books, cooking shows, and cooking classes. There are a number of celebrity chefs on TV, including Emeril Lagasse, Bobby Flay, Caprial Pence, and Sara Moulton. There's even an entire channel, the Food Channel, devoted to cooking and enjoying food.

GenXers are the first generation of adults since two-income families became the norm, and for many that meant breaking the traditional cycle of home-maker mom teaching her daughter how to cook. Christa DiBiase, executive producer of my radio show, says her mother, who was busy with her career, didn't teach her how to cook. But Christa's mother-in-law used to make a home-cooked dinner almost every night for her husband, Mike.

Some GenXers don't want to cook and eat at home. They're perfectly content eating out all the time. But others are finding they want the sense of home that a restaurant can't provide. Eating at home also allows you to control what you eat, making it easier to enjoy meals that are nutritionally better for you.

Christa is pregnant with her first child, and doesn't look forward to taking the baby to restaurants all the time. She says, candidly, that not knowing how to cook "makes me feel kind of inadequate." She's trying to remedy that by taking cooking classes. They're not cheap. Christa paid $60 for a single, hour-long basic cooking class. But learning how to cook just a few meals can save plenty of money over the years.

Of course, you don't have to learn to cook from a chef. If your local community college has a culinary department, that's a great place to look for affordable cooking classes. Some supermarkets offer instruction, to tempt you to buy the ingredients there, and you might find classes that cover certain types of cooking—low-fat or low-salt cooking—at a community center or hospital. Look for smaller classes so you can see what's happening, and if they don't automatically give out the recipes, ask for copies of them.

Cookbooks are an even less expensive alternative. Look in used-book stores or the library for a book that emphasizes basic cooking, find a recipe that looks appealing, and give it a try. The worst thing that can happen in the kitchen is to cut or burn yourself. If you can avoid that, the only thing to worry about is that the food won't taste so good. If it doesn't, try it again and you'll get better at it. Cooking isn't rocket science. If you can read and follow directions, you can figure it out.

Christa says she can make French toast, sandwiches, and pasta. She knows how to make stuffed shells, but the first time she tried it, she didn't realize that you have to boil the pasta shells first, before you stuff and bake them. She remembers thinking, "Why is it so hard to stuff these things?" Live and learn.

Nancy Meltzer, wife of my co-author, Mark Meltzer, is a terrific cook who makes it look easy, and she learned how to cook in her early twenties by watching Julia Child and Graham Kerr, the "Galloping Gourmet," and by reading cookbooks. One of the most frustrating things about picking a recipe out of a book or following one from a TV show, Nancy says, is that recipes may call for a spice or ingredient that a beginning cook doesn't have. It's too expensive to get everything you might need all at once, so Nancy used to buy a new spice at the supermarket every week, and gradually built up her supply. Other dishes might involve a piece of cooking equipment. Making pesto, for example, takes about fifteen minutes. But you can't do it unless you have a food processor, a blender, or a mortar and pestle.

Another thing people have trouble with at first, Nancy says, is cooking a meal so that everything is ready at the same time. If you're serving roast chicken with mashed potatoes and asparagus, the meal doesn't work unless you can serve all of the three foods when they're cooked and hot. That's just a matter of knowing how long it will take to cook each one, and doing a little math.

• Tips on Learning to Cook •

o Cooking classes aren't cheap. A one-hour-long basic cooking class might cost $60 or more. But you'll still save if a class or two can reduce the number of meals you eat in a restaurant.

o You can learn how to cook for less by watching cooking shows or reading cookbooks. Pick up a few cookbooks inexpensively at a used-book store.

* WINE *

It's a great time to be a wine lover.

Winemakers have planted so many new acres of vineyards that there is a massive oversupply of wine, one which probably will last for years. And as basic economics dictates, when there is too much supply and demand remains steady, prices come down.

I don't understand wine at all—to me, it tastes like medicine. But people who drink wine say it's now possible to buy a very good bottle of wine for just $5 to $8. Wine connoisseurs used to say you couldn't buy a good bottle of wine for less than $12. But because of this oversupply, there is very good product, from winemakers in the United States as well as Australia, Chile, and Argentina.

People assume that a $9 bottle of wine will be of higher quality than a $7 bottle, or a $15 bottle will be better than an $8 bottle. But that isn't true. Either might be terrific.

Kim Curley, longtime producer of my radio show and now a wine distributor in Oregon, says people worry too much about the rules of wine drinking, when in fact there aren't any. There are thousands of kinds of wines, and the best ones are the ones that you like. Instead of being intimidated by snobby wine etiquette, try different wines and find kinds that you enjoy.

Kim likes to invite a few friends over for informal wine parties. Each person brings a different bottle, usually priced from $8 to $15. They number each wine, and everybody tastes them to see which ones they like. So for the cost of one bottle, you get to sample six or eight wines. Do that a few times and you'll have a great idea of what kinds of wines you prefer. Kim suggests keeping a "wine journal" you can use to note different wines, and wine characteristics, that you like.

For white wines, Kim likes drier, lighter varieties, such as Pinot Grigio, as opposed to sweeter varieties, like Riesling or Gewürztraminer. For red wine, she prefers Pinot Noir, which is the lightest kind of red wine in color and in flavor. At the opposite end of the reds is cabernet sauvignon, which is aged longer in wood barrels and has a stronger, more intense flavor. Merlot, a red wine many Americans love, has a hint of sweetness.

The Wall Street Journal Guide to Wine is a great guide to the different flavors and characteristics of different varieties of wine. It's a great read.

If you know anything about your own preferences in wine, use them as a guide to trying new wines, and don't worry about price. Most people—70 percent— buy wine because of the look of the label, which is why you see a lot of wine labels with butterflies and beautiful vistas. That won't tell you anything. Wine should be an experiment. If you like it, it's a discovery. If you don't, you've learned something about your tastes.

Where you buy wine is almost as important as what you buy. Buying wine at a discount outlet makes a huge difference. The warehouse clubs have struck fear into traditional wine stores, because they buy in such massive quantities and

mark it up so little that it's possible to get terrific deals.

The cost of wine is affected also by state tax. Florida, for example, charges an excise tax of $2.25 a gallon on wine, while California charges just 20 cents a gallon and New York charges only 19 cents a gallon. The U.S. median is 60 cents a gallon. Other high-tax states include Iowa ($1.75 a gallon), Alabama ($1.70 a gallon), Georgia ($1.51 a gallon), Virginia ($1.51 a gallon), and Hawaii ($1.36 a gallon). Low-tax states include Mississippi, which charges 35 cents a gallon in excise tax on wine, Maryland (40 cents), Kansas (30 cents), and Minnesota (30 cents). People who are really into wine buy it in a low-tax state and bring it home to their higher-tax state. State revenue departments frown on that, but they're not going to bother you if the wine is for personal consumption.

Some states have passed laws prohibiting their residents from buying wine via the Internet. One of those states is Georgia, where I live, and I'm so opposed to that law that, even though I don't drink, I purchased a bottle of wine via the Internet in protest. I bought it during my radio show and told my listeners when it was shipped and when it arrived. Then I opened it during the show, basically challenging the "wine police" to come and arrest me. And nobody ever did. The laws that block online wine sales supposedly are meant to protect young people from buying alcohol illegally. But they're really meant to limit competition and protect profits for local distributors and retailers. Most of the wine you can buy online is high end, priced at as much as $80 a bottle, not the cheap stuff teenagers could afford.

If you buy wine in a restaurant, expect to pay a lot and not get much for it, especially if you buy by the glass. Kim says a lot of middle-market restaurants offer a generic white-red-rosé selection of $5 wines by the glass that are cheaply made, mass-marketed, and not worth drinking. The quality of wine also can be ruined if the bottle has been open for a long time. The *Wall Street Journal* sampled wines from ten major restaurant chains and found half lacking in quality and/or selection, including Applebee's, Chili's, Hooters, Ruby Tuesday, and Bennigan's. The newspaper liked Olive Garden, Romano's Macaroni Grill, and Red Lobster, calling their owners "wine missionaries." The other two, Outback Steakhouse and T.G.I. Friday's, ranked between the three winners and the five low-rated chains.

Kim suggests going to a better restaurant with another couple and sharing a bottle of something nicer.

If you're interested in learning more about wine, check out such magazines as *Wine Enthusiast,* which is introductory, and *Wine Spectator,* which is more advanced. To learn more about how different foods can affect how wine tastes, the magazine *Bon Appétit* can be helpful. The Internet can be helpful, too: www.oregonwine.org and www.wineloverspage.com have a lot of good advice, and so do www.intowine.com and www.epicurious.com. From the book world, there is *Wine for Dummies* and *The Wall Street Journal Guide to Wine.*

• Tips on Wine •

○ You can buy a very good bottle of wine for just $5 to $8.

○ A $15 bottle isn't necessarily better than an $8 bottle. The only way to tell is to try both.

○ Don't be intimidated by snobby wine etiquette. Try different wines and find kinds that you enjoy.

○ Keep a wine journal to note different wines, and wine characteristics, that you like.

○ Sample a number of wines by hosting an informal wine party. Ask each guest to bring a different bottle of wine.

○ Buy wine at discount stores or warehouse clubs, such as Costco, for big savings.

○ Many middle-market restaurants offer a generic selection of $5 wines by the glass that are cheaply made, mass-marketed, and not worth drinking.

• Internet •

www.epicurious.com
www.intowine.com
www.oregonwine.org
www.wineloverspage.com

✳ BOTTLED WATER ✳

I often argue about the virtues of bottled water with Christa DiBiase, executive producer of my radio show. Christa is vehemently opposed to tap water. She just doesn't believe that the government is capable of providing clean drinking water to people.

But most tap water is clean and—here's a surprise—it tastes good. Here in Atlanta, we did a taste test comparing bottled water to tap water for a TV report, and tap water beat bottled. Most of this group of taste testers were avowed bottled-water drinkers, and before the test they went on and on about how they hated the taste of tap water. But in the blind taste test, the tap waters won. The bottled-water drinkers were very surprised that they liked the taste of tap water.

Taste is completely subjective, and you may prefer the taste of bottled water to tap. But taste should be the reason to drink bottled water, not some sense that bottled water is more pure or better for your health than tap. In fact, many of the bottled waters actually come from municipal sources, rather than from some pristine mountain spring.

For the TV report, we tested a variety of tap waters in a lab, and the tests found nothing in the water that would pose any health hazard. It was perfectly safe to drink.

If you live in an area where the water tastes bad, like in many beach communities, bottled water may make more sense. I have a beach home in Florida, and I drink bottled water when I stay there.

Another option is to filter your water, with either a faucet-mounted, refrigerator-mounted, or pitcher-style water filter. *Consumer Reports* magazine (www.consumerreports.org) has tested water filters several times, and found that, while tap water is safe, many filters do a good job of removing "potentially harmful contaminants like lead, parasites, and chlorine by-products such as chloroform." They also do a good job of "removing off-tastes and odors," the magazine says. The downside is the cost of filters, which must be changed every few months. Pitcher-style filters are somewhat cheaper than faucet-mounted filters, but the real cost with either, the cost of filters, is similar. Whichever you choose, it will be cheaper than bottled water.

An alternative is a modified purified-water unit, which looks like a water cooler but really is a refrigerator with a filtration system. The water is filtered and chilled, and it's far cheaper than a traditional bottled-water cooler.

If you do want to buy bottled water, there are some ways to save money. The popularity of bottled water has made it more expensive, but there are a number of private labels that are much cheaper than the top brand names. Wal-Mart sells one called Sam's Choice that costs about twenty cents for a 20-ounce bottle, or about a penny an ounce, whereas expensive bottled waters can cost 3 to 5 cents an ounce. The warehouse clubs have their own private-label waters as well, and they're at or below a penny an ounce for a single-serving size. If you buy a gallon jug, you may get the price below half a penny an ounce.

If you like the portability of a single-serving size, buy one of those and use a gallon jug to refill it.

It doesn't matter what kind of bottled water you buy, as long as you like the taste. So try a few inexpensive varieties first, and if you find one you like, stay with it.

People really get ripped off when they buy a bottle of water at a convenience store, at inflated prices. Instead, keep some in your car, and when you get thirsty, you'll have a bottle nearby. Most people prefer drinking water at room temperature anyway, and it's healthier for your body.

• Tips on Bottled Water •

○ Buy bottled water if you prefer the taste to tap water, not because you think it's more pure or better for your health.

o Try a few inexpensive varieties first, and if you find one you like, stay with it.

o Private labels have some of the best prices.

o Avoid buying bottled water at convenience stores, where it is most expensive.

• Internet •

www.consumerreports.org (Tests on water filters)

CHAPTER 2

FAMILY + CHILDREN

As a father of two children, I can tell you that, while there are challenges to raising children, it's mostly a joy. The greatest challenge is being able to afford them.

Practicality and creativity are key if you're going to have an affordable lifestyle with multiple mouths to feed, bodies to clothe, and minds to educate.

I was very impressed with a couple I met in Raleigh, North Carolina, who have five children, all under the age of fifteen. They have no credit-card debt. Their only debts are a car loan and a mortgage, which is a fifteen-year loan. In addition to being in such a strong financial position, they are happy. "How do you do it?" I asked them. Their answer was they are very practical in raising their children. For example, instead of buying expensive new clothes for each child, they do a lot of hand-me-downs.

In this chapter, I'll show you how to save money when you get ready for your first child, how to raise children with Clark Smart money values, and how to save on braces, private school, and music and dance lessons. I'll also show you how to save when you buy things for those other members of your family, your pets.

✳ BUYING FOR YOUR FIRST CHILD ✳

When a couple finds out they're going to have a child for the first time, there's so much excitement—and so much anxiety.

People often buy too many things in advance—and buy the wrong things—as they try to get ready for their child's first day in their home. Until your child is home, you really don't know what things are going to be useful and what things are not. I have two daughters, and when I think back to what people gave us, I'm surprised at how many of those things we didn't use at all. We even requested some of those items by listing them on a baby registry.

The most practical thing for you to give or receive at a baby shower is gender-neutral clothing, in sizes up to 3T. People give tons of newborn outfits, including some very fancy things that are hard to put on or take off a baby. Fancy clothes end up staying in the closet. What you need are comfortable outfits that are easy to get a child into and out

of, particularly from ages six months to twenty-four months, when the child's size changes rapidly.

Used clothing also is a great idea, because of how fast your child will outgrow everything. Buying new clothes all the time will just eat up your money. If you don't have access to hand-me-downs from friends and family, there are plenty of stores that specialize in selling used children's clothing. Most used baby clothes are in very good condition because they've been used for only a month or so. But check used clothing carefully before you buy. Often these stores have brand-new items as well. If used clothing doesn't appeal to you, try a discounter such as Wal-Mart or Target.

Because of the instability in retailing, a lot of the best deals on clothing are in stores that buy other people's mistakes. Perhaps a department store buyer bought more of an item than the store could handle, or a manufacturer made more of an item than it could sell. Once the season's over, they have to get rid of those goods, so they sell them to stores such as Marshalls, T.J. Maxx, and the ultra-low-cost store Value City, which at this point is in only fifteen states (check www.valuecity.com for locations). Value City's entire business model is based on buying goods from bankrupt manufacturers and retailers and from manufacturers and retailers who simply messed up and bought or made too much of a particular item. They offer reasonable savings during a clothing season, but phenomenal savings after the season. Value City has been a fantastic source for low-priced clothing for my youngest daughter.

Many cities also have no-name liquidators that offer merchandise at huge discounts.

You can always save money on clothes by buying at the right time of the season, no matter where you shop. Don't buy summer clothes in the spring as retailers want you to do; wait until summer actually starts. (See the Cloth-

ing section, in the "Necessities" chapter, for more details.)

The second mistake people often make as they get ready for their first child is they put "baby" furniture in the nursery. It looks so cute, but in just a few years your child isn't going to like being around baby furniture. On the other hand, a toddler is not going to remember what furniture they had as a newborn. So it's more practical to get the things you're going to need—a bassinet, a crib, and a changing table or a changing attachment—and buy traditional furniture. It can be more youth-oriented—but don't buy furniture that works only in a nursery, because it's not going to be around long. You can tell that by how poorly a lot of it is made!

As much as I love secondhand stuff, I want you to be careful with secondhand car seats, cribs, and bassinets, because safety standards change so much through the years. I have two daughters, one born in 1989 and one born in 1999, and it seemed like nothing was the same when my second daughter, Stephanie, was born. Cribs have tighter safety standards. Car seats are completely different. Unless you're doing hand-me-downs for a child born a couple of years earlier, I suggest you buy new.

As for the crib, don't go overboard. I have a friend who spent $800 on his daughter's crib, and when I heard that, I was in shock. Stephanie's crib cost $109, and you really have to work to spend that much. Cribs that meet all safety standards start at around $69. You can get very attractive-looking cribs from $109 to $129. The unnecessary $700 that he spent on a crib could buy a lot of food and diapers.

Christa DiBiase, executive producer of my radio show, bought a crib for her new baby online from Kmart. It looks just like an $800 crib from Pottery Barn, and a friend mistakenly thought she had bought it there. But Christa's cost $180. Too rich for me, but quite a deal nonetheless.

Go to www.safekids.org, the Web site of the National Safe Kids Campaign, for some great safety tips. For example, it says that cribs are required to have no more than 2⅜ inches of space between the slats or spindles, and that a safe crib will have a mattress that fits snugly, covered by a well-fitting crib sheet.

Christa decorated her entire nursery for about $600, and got the look of fancy baby stores and magazines for thousands of dollars less. She went to the flea market and found a great long buffet painted in distressed white. This is "the look" for baby furniture these days, Christa says, but it can be extremely expensive. The cool thing about her "dresser" is that it has two cabinets and three drawers (great for storing baby supplies and clothing). It's much longer than a normal dresser, and easily accommodates a changing pad and supplies on top. It cost her $200, and she has received many compliments on it. If she'd bought it at a retail store, it easily would have cost her $1,500, especially with the distressed look. She can repaint it and use it in a formal dining room once her child outgrows it.

Christa also found a beautiful lamp

and a chandelier for her baby's room at the flea market. The chandelier is in an antique white color, and she bought five different-colored shades she found in an outlet store. It looks like one she saw in a baby store for $800, and she paid a total of $100. Her other flea market finds: great shelves, a cute bookcase made to look like a picket fence, and some prints for the baby's room.

Christa went to a discount store that specializes in home decor and crafts and bought some cute accessories similar to those she saw in a fancy baby store display. She bought a decorative painted birdcage to hold baby supplies in. Cost in baby store: $90. Cost at the home decor discounter: $10. She also bought a white bunny planter to hold Q-tips and a small white watering can to hold cotton balls. Each was $5. The similar accessories in the baby store were $35 each. She also found a great basket to hold baby toys. It cost $10.

For the window treatment, Christa wanted what is called a cornice. She got quotes from two different fabric store vendors and it was going to cost her $200 to have it made by them. Instead, she found a kit and made one herself (no sewing involved—she has no idea how to do that stuff) for $30. These things aren't as hard as they seem. With the leftover fabric, her talented sister-in-law made her a round tablecloth for the $5 side table she found on sale at Kmart.

Christa's nursery looks like a million bucks. She did it by shopping around at some of the expensive baby stores, but leaving her purse at home. You can find some great ideas in their displays and re-create them on your budget. The catalogs also provide an easy way to carry your ideas with you.

Take a similar approach when buying furniture for older children. Kids grow up so fast these days, and their tastes change very quickly. So buying your child an expensive bed that looks like a race car may seem like a great idea when he's four, but he isn't going to want anything to do with it by the time he's eight. When my oldest daughter Rebecca was little, we put these self-sticking cartoon characters on the wall, and she loved them. Then one day, when she was just eight or nine, she said she didn't want them anymore, and we took them down. Why spend a lot of money on furniture that has such a short life cycle? Buy that kind of item at a garage sale.

Baby Formula

Mother's milk is the best nutrient for infants. But a lot of mothers use formula, either exclusively or as a supplement. If you do need formula, you might be surprised to know that generic, or store formula, is exactly the same nutritionally as name-brand formula. In fact, the U.S. Food and Drug Administration sets out the requirements for baby formula, and you can compare them can to can. According to the FDA's Web site (www.fda.gov), "the safety of commercially prepared formula is ensured by the agency's nutrient requirements and by strict quality-control procedures that require manufacturers to analyze each batch of formula for required nutrients, to test

samples for stability during the shelf life of the product, to code containers to identify the batch, and to make all records available to FDA investigators."

One of the big brand names got in trouble for going to doctors' offices and telling them that their formula was better. They were trying to get the doctors to tell patients not to use generic formula. But their claim of superiority wasn't true, and they had to stop using that as a sales pitch.

I spoke with a caller, Annette, who heard me touting generic baby formula on my show. She called me to say that she just wouldn't risk her child's health to save a few bucks. I explained to her that the FDA regulates infant formula, and that if she would just compare the labels on the two canisters of formula, she would see that they are the same. Still unconvinced, Annette asked her pediatrician during her child's checkup appointment. When he told her that the generic formula was equivalent and perfectly fine, she decided to try it. Two weeks later, she called me back to rave about how wonderful the generic formula was, and how much money she was saving. Her child didn't flinch when she switched the formula, and she was able to pocket some money for her little one's future.

Generic formula is usually half the cost of brand-name formula, a bigger discount than other generic products because the stores have to overcome the hesitancy people have about giving generic formula to their child. Just about everybody sells generic formula, from supermarkets to discount stores. It's widely available and a big savings in your budget. Unfortunately, there isn't the same competition on food for older children.

Disposable Diapers

The second big budget-buster for new parents is diapers. People laugh at me because both of my daughters were generic-diaper babies, but again, the savings are gigantic. There's product stratification even in the generic area. So you'll find ultra-discount generics as well as generics whose features and comfort are designed to mimic brand-name disposable diapers. Wal-Mart, for example, has a very inexpensive line of diapers for people who want the rock-bottom low price. We've bought the other, more expensive Wal-Mart brand, which still costs much less than the name brand. We've been thoroughly satisfied.

Even if you buy brand-name diapers, you'll probably try a few different kinds to see which works best for you. So why not try a few generics first? If one variety leaks or irritates your baby's skin, don't buy it again. But if you find a brand that works, you'll save a phenomenal amount of money as you buy diapers, week after week, year after year. Warehouse clubs and supermarkets sell their own brands, as do some drugstores and discount stores.

If you feel guilty about getting generic diapers or formula for your child, put the savings into a college fund and tell your child later that generic diapers put her through college.

• Tips on Buying for Your First Child •

○ Don't buy too many things in advance. Wait until your child is home to see what's going to be useful.

○ Buy comfortable outfits that are easy to get a child into and out of, particularly from ages six months to twenty-four months.

○ Used clothing is a great idea, because of how fast your child will outgrow everything and the practically nonexistent wear and tear.

○ Look for deals on children's clothing in stores that buy other people's mistakes, such as Marshalls, T.J. Maxx, and Value City, which is in only fifteen states.

○ Don't buy "baby" furniture. It won't last long, and in just a few years, your child won't like it.

○ Get ideas from baby stores and catalogs, but re-create their ideas for far less money.

○ Avoid used car seats, cribs, and bassinets. Safety standards change too quickly.

○ If you use baby formula, try generic. It's about half the price of brand-name formula and is required by federal law to be nutritionally equal.

○ Buying generic diapers is another excellent way to save money.

• Internet •

www.safekids.org

www.fda.gov

It's hard to teach children to have good money values. Children often see their parents as the bank, the source of unlimited withdrawals for whatever they want. They don't understand that there are consequences for spending too much money. And they don't understand the idea of making deposits.

Parents have to overcome that by teaching addition and subtraction, and they can do that by using a reward system. The fundamentalist Christian community promoted an idea that's now become more mainstream, and I love it. The idea is to have three jars for money. You give your child a certain amount of money, and it's split among the three jars—spending, saving, and charity. In the fundamentalist model, 10 cents of every dollar goes to charity, and the child gets to choose the charity. So if your child loves animals, you could designate that 10 percent to the Humane Society. The other 90 cents is split in half, with 45 cents going to savings and 45 cents to be spent however the child

wishes. The savings jar could be for a stereo system, a bicycle, or some other long-term goal that eventually will give the child a reward for saving.

The next question is how that money is "earned." Some parents like to give it in exchange for the child completing certain household chores. Others believe the child has a right to share in some of the family's income. Or it could be a combination of both.

When your child reaches his or her early teens and starts earning their own money for baby-sitting or mowing lawns, you can give them an incentive to save by matching every dollar they save. Give them a dollar for every dollar they put into a CD at the bank, instead of a CD at the mall. They'll see that $20 they don't spend becomes $40, and they'll start to understand the benefits of deferred gratification, as opposed to current gratification. In time, they'll become dedicated savers.

Software designer David Hunt has a different approach to this. He created a program called Family Bank (www.parentware.org) that helps teach children ages six to sixteen about money. Parents deposit the child's weekly allowance in an "account," for the child to spend and save. If the child needs more, they can borrow money, but they have to pay it back with interest. So instead of getting $10 a week, they might receive $8.50 a week until the loan is repaid. It's an early lesson in the dangers of credit card abuse.

Hunt's oldest daughter, Alicia, uses Family Bank to manage her clothing budget. So she knows that spending $200 on a pair of Nikes will break the bank, whereas spending $30 on a pair of shoes gives her more options. It's a great idea. When you give a child a set amount of money, or they earn a set amount of money, then you have the rewards and consequences that will help them become a better shopper.

What doesn't work, as I've learned with my thirteen-year-old daughter, Rebecca, is trying to get her to understand that something is too expensive. When I ask, "Do you really need to spend that much on a shirt?" she'll just give me this puzzled look.

At some point between ages eight and twelve, depending on the child, brand-name mania starts to take over the minds of young shoppers. This has been a terrible challenge for me and many other parents, because most children don't understand the consequences of spending so much additional money to wear what the other kids think is "in." It's been a very hard thing for Rebecca. And this is a case when you're going to be unhappy with what I have to say, because we have a "Don't ask, don't tell" rule in the family. I'm not allowed to go on the shopping trips for her clothes now, and I have no idea how much money is being wasted in the name of fashion.

I don't know yet whether Rebecca will become a frugal adult, or anything close.

I do believe strongly that, by teaching a child about money, you can develop an adult who has good money values. When you give a child money again and again, the child never learns the logical consequences of unchecked spending. When they become a young adult, living independently, they pick up the same habits they had living under your roof. That's why you do them an enormous favor teaching them the value of a dollar while they're living with you.

Some parents make the mistake of trying to give their children everything they didn't have when they were children. I know a fellow whose parents were immigrants and had struggled to provide for him. Eventually he did very well financially, and he showered his three children with everything. Whatever they wanted, they got. No one ever said no. Now the three kids are adults, and there's not a dollar they haven't spent.

I talked with a college student once who told me that the money his parents sent him never was enough. And he asked me how he could get his parents to send more. I told him that even if his parents could afford to give him more money to spend on pizza and beer, he couldn't afford to take it. Because if he didn't learn right away that money doesn't come from an unlimited source, he was going to have a lot of trouble in his life.

A lot of parents will buy a brand-new car for their child when he or she turns sixteen, and that's an awful idea. Young drivers are going to get into fender benders, and it's crazy to let them learn these lessons with an expensive new car. It's fine to let the child use the family car, but even better is to provide a child with a recent used car. The child gets the responsibility for gas, maintenance (including oil changes), and insurance. That's a fair amount of money for a teenager, but I think it builds responsibility. When they do get a new car, they'll respect and appreciate it more and take better care of it.

• Internet •

www.parentware.org

✳ MUSIC AND DANCE LESSONS ✳

I wish I had a dollar for every time I got a call from a parent who was upset about signing a contract for karate, music, or dance lessons for his child. Well, maybe I do.

Parents sign these contracts, and then a child's interests quickly change. Or the child might think they want to try karate, and then realize they don't like it. This is a disturbing phenomenon I'm hearing more about with kids. Our children are over-scheduled as it is, and now these places are trying to rope them into long-term agreements before they're even in elementary school.

One of my callers, Karen, wanted to know if she should sign a long-term contract for her son to learn karate. The school she was looking at wanted her to commit her son to a three-year program, which would cost her thousands of dollars over those three years.

The people who run these schools know that what a child is interested in today may not be what they're interested in tomorrow. The school has an incentive to get the parents to sign, so that, whether or not the child sticks with the lessons, the school still gets its money.

Schools like this also go out of business frequently, so your money is at risk if you pay in advance. Even if the school is financially strong, the service you receive will be better if the school has an incentive to earn your money and your loyalty. If you have already agreed to pay them for three years, there is no incentive for them to do a great job.

I strongly encouraged Karen to look elsewhere for a karate school that would both teach her son and earn her business month after month.

It's great to want to enrich your children by getting them involved in some cultural or physical activity, but it's important to know that your money is at risk. If you can find a place that will let you pay lesson-by-lesson, that's the way to go.

Sometimes your city or county will

have good programs available, and they're never going to involve a contract. You pay a lot of money in taxes, so why not take advantage? Schools often have after-school programs that provide an affordable way for you to try something new for your child.

A lot of privately run schools won't take your child unless you sign a contract. They're okay to consider, but don't sign a contract for any longer than six months. That's a long time in a child's life. A year is too long.

Don't rely on the salesperson or the sales literature to decide whether a place is good for your child. Ask other parents which places they've had good experiences with.

• Tips on Lessons •

○ Look for enrichment programs that don't require you to sign a contract. If you have to sign a contract to enroll, don't agree to a term of longer than six months.

○ Check with your city or county to see if they offer such programs.

○ Schools often have after-school programs that provide an affordable way for you to try something new for your child.

✳ THE DENTIST ✳

The advice you get from a dentist, or any doctor, may not always be correct.

I did a TV report a few years ago that showed just what a variety of opinions you can get. We took a "patient" who had absolutely nothing wrong with her to six different dentists, complaining of a toothache. What they recommended was unbelievable, ranging from major invasive work to the best answer: that she was just fine and might be having a temporary problem.

My nephew had problems with his teeth, and the dentist his parents trusted went as far as to wire his mouth shut for six months. It turned out that it not only wasn't what he needed—it was the wrong thing.

I get a lot of calls from people asking about the prices dentists charge. But what I've learned is that price isn't the most important factor in dentistry. Although dentistry is a science and a skill, there's also a lot of art involved. There's a range of opinions as to what the right treatment is for a particular patient. If a dentist recommends a root canal and people trust the dentist or orthodontist they go to, they say okay. But that's not what you should do. If a dentist recommends a serious treatment for you, it is so important for you to get a second, even a third opinion. I don't care if the dentist is a family friend or the dentist your family has been going to for three generations.

Go get a second opinion before major work is done.

We've had calls from people who have root canals done who were told later that they weren't necessary. One fellow I spoke with went to a dentist to have a gap in his teeth closed, and wound up having more than $10,000 in unnecessary dental work done. The dentist convinced him that it would be better to wear a bridge than to wear braces to correct the problem. The doctor pulled several teeth that he had not told his patient were going to be pulled, and the bridge ended up being a poor fit—it was very uncomfortable and loose. So the dentist then removed that bridge and replaced it with another one, which didn't work either. Finally, the fellow had to go to another dentist to have the bridge removed and have another one put in. The second dentist told him that braces would have been fine for him, and that he should not have gone through this as a twenty-one-year-old.

I had a caller once who was one of the most thorough consumers I've ever spoken with. She took her child to five different orthodontists, and their unanimous opinion was that the child needed braces. The range of prices she was quoted was huge, and she couldn't figure out which orthodontist was the right one to use. She was worried that the lowest-priced orthodontist was going to cut corners and do inferior work, so she was thinking of choosing the mid-priced orthodontist. I told her to get a written description from each orthodontist of what they were going to do, and if the descriptions seemed equivalent, choose the lowest-priced provider. I never heard back from her, but it surprised me that such a thorough consumer would be willing to pay more without a good reason.

If you live in a large city, you should expect to pay $5,000 to $7,000 for your child's braces, less in a smaller city. The more complicated the treatment, the more expensive it's likely to be. Braces for an adult could cost more or less. If an adult just wants to uncrowd some lower teeth, it could run $1,000 or less for a simple retainer. But if the work is extensive, an adult could pay 50 percent more than a child. Since an adult's jaw

is no longer growing, moving teeth takes more time and adds cost. An adult might need to wear braces for three years for the same treatment that could be done on a child in two. Adults also tend to prefer invisible orthodontia, which is more exotic and more expensive—perhaps 50 percent more than the regular kind.

It's a good idea to see what, if anything, your insurance may cover. Some policies may pay no more than $1,500 for braces. Others may not pay for braces for anyone over age twenty-one.

Cosmetic dentistry is big business today as well, particularly teeth whitening. But you don't need expensive dental treatments to whiten your teeth. We tried an over-the-counter product, Crest Whitestrips, and they worked great. They cost about $34 for a series of treatments. You place this clear film over your teeth and it does a good job of whitening as long as you stick with it. Only one of our staffers, a heavy smoker, got no results. The Whitestrips couldn't overcome the yellowing effect of heavy smoking. But for most people, the only reason they'd need to go to the dentist for teeth whitening is if they don't have the discipline to follow the at-home regimen.

If you're using the Crest Whitestrips, it's good to have your teeth cleaned first by a dentist, so you don't end up bleaching the plaque on your teeth, according to J. Crystal Baxter, a Chicago prosthodontist (reconstructive dentist). Dr. Baxter loves a new laser bleaching system dentists are using. It does a remarkable job in a single one-hour treatment, although it costs $600 to $800 to whiten all your teeth. Bleaching your teeth at home with a professional kit from a dentist can cost $300 to $500. I say try the Crest product for $34, and see if it works for you.

Dentists shift to cosmetic dentistry because the number of cavities people have been getting has been declining over the years. But the dental health of adolescents is declining again, in part because children and teenagers are drinking so-called sports drinks instead of water. Kids have been drinking soft drinks for quite a while. Sports drinks have made it worse,

and that's harming their teeth. So dentists may have a big business in repairing tooth decay again in the future.

One thing parents can do to protect their children's teeth is have them sealed. The procedure seals tiny cracks and fissures in the tooth's surface, so they don't get cavities. It costs about $50 to $70 per tooth and lasts about five or six years. It's an excellent value, because preventing cavities now can save your children from expensive crowns and root canals later.

Some people are electing to have their silver-mercury amalgam fillings replaced, fearing that they may suffer harm from the toxic mercury in the fillings. Dr. Baxter says the mercury in those fillings is inert, and she's seen no definitive proof that it causes any harm. Having them removed should be considered only if you've had immune system problems, she says.

People ask about the price of dentistry because so much of it is uninsured. Even people who have dental insurance find it far less thorough than regular health insurance. For example, a policy might have a $1,200 annual limit, and provide only a 50 percent reimbursement for a $600 or $700 crown. If you think you may have more significant dental expenses in a year and have access to a flexible spending plan at work, you could use that to trim your costs. As I point out in the section on prescription drugs, flexible spending plans allow you to pay medical costs out of gross, or before-tax, dollars, so you get a substantial discount, usually 30 percent or more. You ask your employer to take a specified amount of money out of each paycheck, and you use that money to pay for dental work that isn't paid by the company health plan. So if you need a $700 crown and insurance will pay $350, you can pay the other $350 from the flexible spending plan. Since $350 of your gross pay might be equal to $250 or less of your net pay, you save $100 or more. But you have to ask to have the money taken out of your paycheck before the year begins, and if you don't spend it by year-end, you lose it. For that reason, flexible spending works best when you can predict your expenses in advance. Ask your dentist for an estimate of the next year's expenses, and ask your employer to place that amount into your flexible spending account.

• Tips on Dentistry •

○ Get a second opinion before undergoing any major dental work.

○ If you want to whiten your teeth, try Crest Whitestrips before you consider professional bleaching. But get your teeth cleaned first. It doesn't work well for smokers.

○ Consider getting your children's teeth sealed to prevent cavities.

- Don't get silver-mercury amalgam fillings replaced. The mercury in the fillings hasn't been shown to cause any harm.

- If you have access to a flexible spending plan at work, you can use it to save on dental expenses.

✳ PRIVATE SCHOOLS ✳

You may be wondering why, in a "book of bargains," I would have anything about private schools, one of the most expensive choices parents can make regarding their children. I think a private-school education is one of the biggest bargains, because of the benefit you get in developing your child's skills and earning power from sending your child to private school. Sometimes, very rarely, you have to spend money to have a big payoff, and this is one of those cases.

Whether you prefer a public school, private school, or a charter school, or even if you homeschool, there is nothing that's right for every member of your family. Schools, like people, have personalities. So the school you loved as a child or the one that worked so well for one of your children might not be best for another.

My wife and I went to both public and private schools and my older daughter, Rebecca, went to public school for several years and now is in private school. Rebecca applied to six private schools and was fortunate to be accepted at five. So we had to figure out which one of the five would be best for her. I knew Rebecca would do best at a school that had more freedom and less conformity, while I can tell already that it's going to be just the opposite for my younger daughter, Stephanie, who's just two and a half. My brother, Neal, was thrown out of a school in eighth grade and ended up going to a military school. It was a perfect fit for him, just an ideal environment, and he flourished there. It was an experience that has benefited him all of his life, and he's fifty-two now. But if you had put me in a military school, it would not have been the best fit at all.

Believe it or not, there are a lot of parents who now hire consultants to figure out what school would be best for their child. These consultants conduct psychological and academic tests and try to find the right school for your child.

Judith Greenberg, an educational consultant and "advocate for students," says you evaluate any school, public or private, by determining how your child would fit in, educationally and socially. Are classes too large? Is your child a different kind of learner? Many schools have a kind of conveyor-belt mentality, Greenberg says. If your child can read about Argentina six times in a book but doesn't understand unless he draws a map of South America, he will be lost in a school that doesn't have a hands-on approach. If you have to fight with teachers and officials constantly about how to educate your child, it's time to get out, Greenberg says.

On the social side, Greenberg has found that kids who don't fit in, who have no friends, or become victims of bullying won't be able to learn.

Not surprisingly, Greenberg says educational consultants can be very helpful. Some test your child and help with the application process. Others are very good at measuring the personality of a school to see if your child will be comfortable. Consultants cost about $600 to $1,200. You can find one by searching for "educational consultants" or "private school consultants" at your favorite search engine.

If you're really lost and don't have that intuitive feel for what would be best for your child, it's okay to hire a consultant. But I think most parents can do this on their own. Whether you're considering a private or public school, get permission to visit the school and observe for half a day. You'll pick up the atmosphere quickly. Some parents will go to an open house at the school, but that's an artificial atmosphere. Just go on a regular classroom day and figure out if you think your child will do well in that environment.

Looking back, I know that the public school Rebecca was in, although it's fantastic academically, wasn't a good environment for her. If I'd known then what I know now, I would have moved her.

There are plenty of private-school options for parents. Many parents put their child in public school through the elementary and middle school years, and then move them to a private high school. Others choose private school from first grade, or go with public school the whole way. I don't like how school systems—to supposedly become more cost efficient—are moving kids into gigantic schools as early as sixth grade. Kids get lost in the education factory. It seems to me that public education does fine at the elementary-school level, but it fails children when schools become warehouses.

Private school isn't cheap. It ranges from $3,000 to $16,000 a year for day schools, more for boarding schools. High school tends to cost more than elementary school because there are more public elementary schools and thus more competition to hold down the tu-

ition. Generally, the Catholic-affiliated schools have the lowest tuition, if you're a member of the church and the school is small.

One way to assess the quality of a school is to see how many of the students stay through graduation. At Rebecca's school, 85 percent stay to graduation, a very high rate. Greenberg, the educational consultant, says you should ask a school where its students go after leaving. For example, if a school ends at third grade, what school does it feed into? If it ends at eighth grade, what high school does it feed into? If a high school, what colleges did the students who graduated in the last few years go to? Ask for the school's SAT scores and the results of other standardized tests. But don't get hung up on accreditation, she says. Some very good small schools find it too costly to seek accreditation.

Some parents—about 2 percent nationally—are skipping both public and private schools and electing to teach their children at home. The winner of a recent National Geographic Bee was homeschooled, as was the third-place winner and 22 percent of the national finalists.

Some people look at parents who homeschool their children as weird or cultlike, but I think it's a perfectly valid way to educate your child, if you have the time and patience to do it. A survey by the U.S. Department of Education found that nearly half (48.9 percent) chose homeschooling because they thought they could give their children a better education at home. Of those surveyed, 38.4 percent cited religious reasons and 25.6 percent said there was a poor learning environment at school. Other factors cited were family reasons (16.8 percent), the chance to develop character/morality (15.1 percent), objections to what school teaches (12.1 percent), the opinion that school does not challenge child (11.6 percent), other problems with available schools (11.5 percent), student behavior problems at school (9.0 percent), and child has special needs/disability (8.2 percent). Parents were allowed to choose multiple answers.

A lot of people look at homeschooling as an either/or matter. But what's happening around the country is that parents are doing a hybrid of school and homeschooling. The children go to school, perhaps, to study the sciences, and the parents teach the rest of the curriculum at home. Or the child may want to participate in a competitive sport. So they attend high school part-time. Schools have a financial incentive to cooperate with this, because they receive more funding for each child who attends.

There's even a school now that doesn't want to be called a school. It's a resource center for homeschooled kids.

Another avenue for some parents is private "learning centers" that provide extra help for children with their studies. Some parents use these centers because they feel guilty that they can't afford to put their child in private school. That's the wrong reason. Use a learning center if your child needs one.

I had a call from one parent who couldn't afford private school or the high cost of a private learning center. I passed along a suggestion I got from a teacher: Find a student who is studying education in college, a junior- or senior-level student, and hire them to help your child. Call a nearby college that offers education degrees. A college student can earn experience in their field and earn $8 to $10 an hour at the same time.

Some people think that anything that changes the educational system is harmful to the idea of universal education. Free public education is a strong part of our society. But options are what create innovation, which strengthens all forms of education. Don't get stuck in a rut where you think the only place for your child is in a private school, or a public school, or homeschool. Keep your perspective. This isn't about philosophy. It's about your child, and you always should keep in mind what's best for your child.

• Tips on Private Schools •

○ Schools have personalities. So the school you loved as a child or that worked so well for one of your children might not be best for another.

○ Evaluate any school, public or private, by determining how your child would fit in, educationally and socially.

○ If you don't have that intuitive feel for what would be best for your child, it's okay to hire an educational consultant to help.

○ Private school ranges from $3,000 to $16,000 a year for day schools, more for boarding schools.

○ If your child needs extra help in school, call a local college that offers education degrees and hire a junior- or senior-level student as a tutor.

✳ PETS ✳

Every time a new movie comes out that features a particular breed of dog, people rush out to get one. It happened with Disney's *101 Dalmatians* and with *Snow Dogs*, which starred a pack of Siberian huskies.

The sad part is when the new owners realize that either they're not dog people or they don't like the personality traits or needs of that particular dog. Dalmatians, for example, are very lively, probably too much so for very young children. They need a lot of exercise. Huskies shed their thick coats at least once a year and like to dig. And they're friendly with strangers, so they don't make good guard dogs. Many of the dogs the owners return end up in shelters, waiting to be put to sleep, or with rescue societies who take them in.

The American Kennel Club (www.akc.org) publishes a book, *The AKC's Complete Dog Book*, that describes the characteristics of each breed. Look for a copy at the library, or look for information online. The Web site www.about-dogs.com has a table that lists the size, coat length, activity level, temperament, and other qualities of various dog breeds. For example, if you want a dog that is tolerant of children, you might consider a beagle, border collie, or golden retriever, but rule out a German shepherd, Jack Russell terrier, or Pekingese. If you want a small dog that isn't too hyperactive for an apartment or small house, you could choose a Boston terrier, a Maltese, or a dachshund.

If you truly want to own a purebred dog, one of the best things you can do, both for the world and for your wallet, is to go to one of the rescue societies for that breed. You get the best of both worlds. Instead of writing a big check for a purebred dog, you get one for free. And you provide a loving home for an unwanted dog. There are rescue societies for virtually every breed.

When you get a purebred dog from a rescue society, it may or may not have papers, the documents that establish its lineage. Unless you're going to breed for profit, that shouldn't matter.

If you're not a breeder, and very few people should be, please spay or neuter it. Dogs that are spayed or neutered live longer, healthier lives, and doing this helps reduce pet overpopulation. The Humane Society of the United States estimates that 8 to 10 million dogs and cats enter shelters each year and 3 to 5 million are put to sleep. The Humane Society says one female cat and her offspring theoretically can produce 420,000 cats in seven years.

There's nothing wrong with having a mixed-breed dog—in fact, there are a lot of good reasons to own one. Just as breeding can enhance certain desirable traits in purebreds, it also can enhance undesirable traits. Mixed-breeds benefit from their genetic diversity. Instead of being one of many, your mixed-breed could be one of a kind.

You can get a mixed-breed at the Humane Society or shelter in your city. You'll take a dog that probably doesn't have much of a future and create a loving home environment.

Most of the complaints I get are from people who buy dogs, either from a pet store or a dog breeder or broker. A lot of the people who pretend to be breeders actually are just brokers, selling the dog on behalf of a breeder.

I had one caller who had some serious problems with a pedigreed puppy he bought from a pet shop. The dog turned out to be sick and didn't have the proper papers. The pet store told him that his papers were simply lost, and that they didn't have any knowledge of the puppy's illness. The pet shop owner was conveniently absent whenever he went back in to discuss the problems with his dog, and his calls were not returned. Finally, he spoke with the mall management office where the shop was located, and was able to get some pressure put on the pet store. He received a credit for the missing paperwork, but still had to shell out big bucks to make his dog well again. This pet store was likely buying from a puppy mill, where dogs are kept in deplorable conditions and bred for the sole purpose of a quick profit. They are often taken away from their mothers early (less than eight weeks), and might be abused or neglected.

A real dog breeder is someone who loves animals, and because they do, they will take the dog back and give you a full refund if it doesn't work out for you. They won't want an animal to be in a situation that isn't best for the animal. Brokers and pet stores have the opposite policy. All sales are final, as soon as you purchase the dog. No refunds. That's how you'll be able to tell someone who is a fellow animal lover versus someone who is a lover of money. If you can't bring the animal back for a full refund, that's the wrong place to buy.

It's always tough to have to return an animal, but it happens. Sometimes a dog that seems perfect in the shelter isn't a good fit with the rest of the family. Maybe he's too destructive, and training can't fix the bad behavior. Or maybe he doesn't get along with your child or another pet.

If it isn't going to work out, try to decide as soon as you can, because it's not fair to the animal to keep it six months,

let it get comfortable in its new home, and then return it. A relative of mine took in a dog that someone else had been unable to make a good home for, and it turned out the animal had psychological problems. She tried, but it didn't work out for her either. She returned the animal in two weeks.

Regardless of where you get your new animal, take it to the veterinarian right away, to make sure it is healthy. If a dog has advanced heartworm or hip dysplasia or some other serious illness, it's best to find out right away.

Before you adopt a dog, do some advance planning to increase your chances of success. If you have children or plan to, don't buy a breed of dog that doesn't live well with children. If you're not sure if you are a dog person, pet-sit for a friend's dog while they're on vacation.

Look over your budget and make sure you can afford the cost of food, annual shots, heartworm prevention, flea control medication, and an occasional trip to the vet to treat an illness. Pets can be expensive, and if you're not willing to shoulder the expense, don't get one.

Never buy a pet for another person as a gift, because that's a recipe for failure. They may not like the kind of dog or cat you think they would like. Many shelters prohibit taking a pet for someone else, even for a child, for just this reason. It's why a lot of rabbits are brought to shelters after Easter and a lot of kittens come in after Christmas. If you want to buy your child a pet as a gift, buy him or her a stuffed dog or cat to represent the gift, then take your child to the shelter to pick out a pet they click with.

With other kinds of animals, such as birds, find out how long this kind of animal usually lives. Some varieties of parrots, for example, live for eighty years or more. Can you commit to keeping a pet for such a long time?

The Humane Society says people should not keep wild animals, such as exotic birds and reptiles, as pets. Some are illegal to own, or simply don't make good pets. According to the organization's Web site, www.hsus.org, "They often grow to be larger, stronger and more dangerous than owners expect or can manage." And they can carry diseases or parasites that can be dangerous to people. My veterinarian, Dr. Nicholas W. Petty, said that decades ago, a couple brought him an ocelot they were keeping as a pet. An ocelot is a twenty-five- to thirty-pound wildcat that bites and urinates straight backward. The guy had wounds on his arms, and as Dr. Petty said, "These people had no friends."

Pet Food

Lane and I have two dogs: Costco Wholesale and Q.T. (named after the regional discount gas retailer QuikTrip). The deal was that Lane got to have dogs if I got to name them. If we get a third, I'll probably call it Charles Schwab, or Chuck for short.

Costco has eaten inexpensive store-brand dog food her whole life (she's six) and has always been very healthy. Q.T., on the other hand, has always had health problems, and goes from one vet-ordered special diet to another. She costs as much to feed as a human being.

It's a riot, because one dog must cost 10 cents a day to feed, and the other $10.

If you have a healthy dog, I think it's just fine for you to feed it store-brand food, until a problem presents itself, because the savings through the years are so gigantic. Any pet food that has AAFCO (Association of American Feed Control Officials) on its label will meet the complete nutritional needs of your pet. Pet food is regulated by the U.S. Food and Drug Administration, by each state, and by AAFCO and the U.S. Department of Agriculture.

Mark Meltzer used to feed his dogs a brand of dog food that's sold in supermarkets, until both developed kidney stones. The dogs went on an expensive vet-ordered low-magnesium diet, and the kidney stones went away. Mark didn't want to put them back on the food he believes contributed to the kidney stones, but he didn't want to keep them on the vet's expensive food forever. So he switched to one of the pet-store brands, and never had another problem.

Dr. Petty says some inexpensive foods can bring on skin problems in some dogs, and he says cheap foods can contain more fillers, meaning the dog would have to eat more to get the same nutrition. That could mean the dog would have larger stools.

Whatever brand you choose, dry dog food is much cheaper than canned food. My dog Costco, appropriately, eats Costco's private-label brand of dry dog food.

Pet Health Insurance

Pets, like people, get sick, and caring for them can be expensive. I just paid the vet $472 to treat my dog Q.T. for pancreatitis, an intestinal disorder.

One of the ways to deal with the rising cost of pet health care is to buy health insurance for your pet. Veterinarians encourage you to buy pet insurance because they realize that a lot of people are in a money crunch. The procedures the vet can perform on animals—surgery, X-rays, and other treatments—can be very expensive but potentially life-saving for your pet. A lot of people have to make an economic choice. They may not be able to afford a treatment that could save their pet's life. That's where pet insurance enters the picture. It may not necessarily save you money, but it gives you the option to do more heroic medical procedures for your animal. For example, the vet wants a radiologist to do an ultrasound of Q.T.'s pancreas. That's going to cost an unbelievable amount of money. If such a procedure would have been impossible otherwise, it is possible with pet insurance. So like other kinds of insurance, it gives you peace of mind.

The pet insurance industry has been improving in quality and in its offerings. Insurers vary in the quality of coverage and claims processing. Yet, perhaps because it once was just about useless, only about 1 percent of pet owners buy pet insurance.

The best way to find a good pet insurance company is to ask your vet which insurance their customers have had the best results with. Premiums for pet insurance start at about $10 a month per pet, and are based on the type of pet, its age, and the type of insurance plan you choose. Some plans cover major illnesses only, while others also include routine vaccinations, heartworm prevention, and flea control medication.

I'm neutral about pet insurance. It makes sense if you would be financially or emotionally crushed if your pet became seriously ill and you had to decide between two terrible outcomes. If you're interested, ask your vet what plans he or she likes, and which one customers have had a good experience with.

A great way to save on pet medicines is to visit PetCareRX.com, an online pet pharmacy. For example, Heartgard Plus, a chewable heartworm prevention medicine, costs $19.77 on PetCareRX.com versus $34.44 at PetsMart. Advantage flea killer for dogs costs $32 on PetCare RX.com, and PetsMart charges $40.02.

• Tips on Pets •

○ If you want a purebred dog, get one from one of the rescue societies for the breed you like.

○ There are a lot of good reasons to own a mixed-breed dog. Get one at the Humane Society or shelter in your city.

○ Inexpensive store-brand food should be fine for most animals. Make sure it has AAFCO (Association of American Feed Control Officials) on its label, your assurance that it will meet the complete nutrition needs of your pet. Dry food is cheaper.

○ I'm neutral on pet health insurance. It makes sense if you would be financially or emotionally crushed if your pet became seriously ill.

○ Save money on pet medicines at www.PetCareRX.com

• Internet •

www.hsus.org
www.PetCareRX.com
www.about-dogs.com

CHAPTER 3

NECESSITIES

Of all the things we spend money on each month, some could be considered things we need, and some could be considered things we don't need. But the distinction between the two isn't that easy to make.

What must we buy? Well, we have to wear clothes every day and have shoes on our feet. If we get sick, we may need a prescription medicine to help us get better.

Other products or services, such as a haircut or cosmetics, are less necessary, but have become an important part of today's lifestyle. In this chapter, I'll show you some strategies to save money on some of the necessities of life, and others you may think of as necessities.

I'll also show you how to save on something I wear every day but hate: eyeglasses. Or, if you can stand putting them in your eyes, I'll show you how to save on contact lenses.

We may need to get dressed every day, but we certainly don't need the amount of clothes that many people own. I once bought a house that was built in 1937, and the closet in the master bedroom was barely larger than the door. In those days, ten outfits might be all a couple owned. Now those ten outfits might be enough for two people for a week.

As you read this chapter, think about some of the things that have become necessities, that really are optional, and be flexible in how you spend in many of these areas.

✳ CLOTHING ✳

As frugal as I am about everything else, I'm extra cheap when it comes to clothing. I recently broke the $10 shirt "barrier" when I paid $12.96 for a dress shirt at Wal-Mart. It was the first time I paid more than $9.99.

I used to buy irregular dress shirts, but the last few times I went shopping, I couldn't find the selection I wanted in the irregulars, so I had to spend a little more.

Clearly, I don't buy what the stores call "fashion forward" clothing, because I believe today's trend is tomorrow's donation to Goodwill. Some people might consider that dull. Others might say I prefer classic styles. I accept dull, because dull is more affordable.

But even if, like most people, you spend more on clothes than I do, I have some wonderful strategies that can help you cut how much you pay.

A great way to save is to buy at the right time of the season. Retailers are always out ahead of the weather. They put spring clothes out during winter, fall clothes during summer, and winter clothes during fall. If you buy ahead of the season, as the retailers want you to, you're going to pay too much. But if all you do is wait until the actual season to buy, you'll save a tremendous amount of money, as retailers mark down the merchandise in order to move it. Retailers refer to spring clothes that are still for sale during spring as past-season goods. For them, the season is already over. This technique works no matter how much you normally spend.

Where you buy your clothes can help you save as well. The clothing market has shifted away from the traditional department stores to specialty retailers, because people want both fashion and low prices. That trend has helped fuel the rise of Kohl's and Target, two stores that have found the right blend of fashion and price that consumers want.

Target, for example, sells very stylish clothes, including a brand called Mossimo which used to be sold only by high-end retailers. Sonja Kashuk, a well-known makeup artist, has her own line of cosmetics at Target; women rave that her products are as good as those sold at expensive makeup counters in department stores.

But even with discounters such as Target and Kohl's, you can save a substantial amount of money if you follow the calendar.

When my wife and I first met, saving money on clothes just wasn't a concern to her. But she picked up a few things from me, and now the student has become the master. She is absolutely fantastic. She has a wonderful eye for fashion and she's very patient. She'll even buy true past-season clothes, stuff that goes all the way to the bargain rack. Summer may be over, but she'll buy the good stuff that's left on the rack knowing she can wear it next summer. She doesn't try to buy a whole wardrobe, because the selection at that point is limited, but if she sees something that will fit into her wardrobe, she buys it. It's been a fascinating transformation.

You can get some great deals if you are willing to buy something you may not wear until next year. A leather jacket you buy at the end of winter could be half off its original price— maybe more—and you'll wear it year after year. Pick up next year's swimsuits and shorts at the end of summer. Are shorts going to go out of style?

One problem a lot of people have with clothes is they buy something and then never wear it. I have some shirts I bought and then never wore, even though buying them seemed like a good decision at the time. Buying clothes is both a practical and an emotional decision, and you're going to make mistakes. There's really no good solution to it.

Men often are reluctant clothing buyers, especially when it comes to suits. We're worried how we're going to look in a suit. People wonder whether it's okay to go to one of the discount clothing stores such as Men's Wearhouse, K&G, or S&K. I have purchased suits from discounters and have been absolutely thrilled with the quality. I routinely pay $100 to $130 and the suits look great. I've never bought one that I've been embarrassed to wear. I've also purchased used suits and been happy with them, and the best deals for men on used clothing are the dressy clothes. A lot of guys will buy a suit and then gain weight, so they'll get rid of the suit. A used suit will cost very little. I bought one for just $1, and the most I've paid is $25. I wore a suit for a TV commercial that I had bought for $2.75 at a Goodwill store in Dayton, Ohio. The savings are tremendous. And many of these suits have never been worn.

I was giving a speech to a military trade association, and when I arrived and opened my suitcase, I realized that my suit wasn't there. I had left it on the bed back home. The speech was that evening and I knew people were going to be decked out in their best clothes. Going in my tennis shorts and dress shoes wasn't an option. So I pulled out the local phone book and started driving around to used-clothing stores. I had to go to three, and in the third one I found a really nice suit for $6. So I mentioned it in my speech. About five minutes into my speech, I asked the person who introduced me to stand next to me, and I asked him how he liked my suit. He liked it a lot, and was surprised when I told him how little it cost. After the speech, people were coming up to me, one after another, to look at my suit.

Buying used clothing can be a great way to save money. One of my producers, Kimberly Drobes, wears very nice clothing—she favors vintage, 1950s-style clothes—and she buys about 70 percent of her outfits used. Kimberly goes "thrifting" regularly at her favorite used-clothing stores. On one trip, she bought a cotton dress for $3.99, a button-down shirt for $1.99, a handbag for $2, and a pair of jeans for $4.99. Her friend bought dresses for $3.99 and $4.99, and a pair of jeans for $5.99. Kimberly says thrifting is hit or miss. Some days she comes back with an armful of clothes, sometimes nothing, so it's not a good way to shop for a specific item. Some used clothes are so worn they're nearly mutilated, Kimberly says, while others still have the price tag on them. So you have to look for something that suits you.

When you buy new clothes, you don't know how well they're made or whether they will hold up over time. Used clothes have already passed that test. When I buy a used sportcoat or suit, I turn it inside out and check to see if any of the seams have ripped, to make sure it's in good shape. It's funny, but most of the time I have trouble with something like a broken zipper if it's on a new item, not a used item. I bought a past-season leather jacket for $49 and

the zipper broke. So it wasn't that well made. A used jacket would have stood the test of time.

You can find local used-clothing stores in the Yellow Pages under "Thrift Stores." Some cities have local chains. Chicago, for example, has City Discount Thrift. Salvation Army and Goodwill stores also are places where you can find good used clothing.

Buying used clothes is an especially good idea for young, growing children, because their sizes change so quickly. Buying new clothes for a child is very expensive. Some parents think it's beneath them to put used clothes on their child. So what I recommend is, go look for a nearly new item for yourself, something you would be proud to wear. Buy it and wear it, and if you get past your reluctance for yourself, maybe you'll be able to get past your reluctance to buy used clothes for your child.

One fun place to pick up some great used stuff is from the unclaimed baggage center in Boaz, Alabama. I bought a beautiful Lord & Taylor men's overcoat for $65 that looked like it had never been worn. Someone had left it in an overhead bin on an airplane, and it ended up in Boaz. People generally travel with their nicest clothes, and when baggage gets lost or things are left behind on an airplane, the airlines wait thirty days to try to reunite them with their owners. Then they go to the unclaimed baggage center to be sold.

Outlet Stores

Outlet stores have been touted as a great way to save, but a lot of that reputation comes from long ago, when factory outlet stores really were attached to the factory, and the bargains they sold either were irregulars or were goods that had been returned because the retailer had gone out of business. I used to buy dress shirts at an Arrow factory outlet for $2 to $6. The $6 shirts were great. They might have had an irregularity in the shirttail that wasn't visible when I wore it. The $2 shirt might have had a tear in the sleeve. That kind of clothing is more appropri-

ate to wear when you're painting the bedroom.

Outlet stores today, conveniently located by an Interstate exit next to 150 other stores, are not true outlets. They're shopping malls, and the merchandise sold at this sort of outlet usually isn't a bargain. Modern outlets have proliferated because department stores, trying to prevent comparison shopping, sell more private-label merchandise than ever before. That has forced the brand-name manufacturers to create their own stores to sell their goods.

If you're really sold on a brand name or a designer, the selection at an outlet will be far superior to what you'll see at a department store. But the prices won't be any better. Modern outlets actually have split into three sectors—stores that sell lower-priced goods, stores that sell mid-priced merchandise, and stores that sell high-end merchandise.

The deals in an outlet store are not the merchandise that's well displayed at the front of the store. The bargains— mostly irregulars or past-season merchandise—usually are in the back of the store, maybe even in a separate room. So if you shop outlets, walk past the high-priced stuff and look for the deals.

Going-Out-of-Business Sales

When you see a sign that says a local store is going out of business and marking everything way down, be careful. Most going-out-of-business sales are rip-offs, because instead of selling the remaining merchandise in the store for less, the store sells all of its merchandise in one transaction to a liquidator. The liquidator then brings in all kinds of new merchandise, and marks it with supposedly big discounts. It might bring in a sofa that supposedly was $1,400 before the store had to sell out, and now sells for $300. But the sofa never sold for $1,400. It was brought in to make money during the liquidation. In a given liquidation, this sort of "fake merchandise" might make up 20 to 80 percent of everything being sold.

If you're going to shop at a going-out-of-business sale, shop only for merchandise that you have an opportunity to compare to similar merchandise in other stores, or for things that you know well enough to be able to determine whether the 60-percent-off "sale" price is hype or a true bargain.

Some stores are constantly "going out of business" but never actually close. That's a deceptive business practice that is illegal in most states. Oriental rug shops have become infamous for pulling these fake going-out-of-business sales. Most states now limit such sales to a certain number of days, and require that the store close at the end of the sale. But these laws are widely abused. Obviously, you should stay away from fake going-out-of-business sales.

Online Coupons

Coupons are a great way to save money, and you can find online coupons very easily. Go to your favorite search engine and search for "coupon code" and you'll see a variety of Web sites with discount offers. If you see a deal you like, maybe for free shipping, use the special coupon code like you would a paper coupon.

• Tips on Clothing •

○ Wait until the season actually begins, rather than before the season, when retailers want you to buy.

○ Skip the department store and try fashion-oriented discounters such as Kohl's or Target.

○ Men can buy good-quality suits at discounters such as Men's Wearhouse, K&G, and S&K for $100 to $130.

○ Save by buying nearly new used clothing.

○ Be careful at outlet stores. There are very few bargains, and those are usually in the back of the store.

○ Most going-out-of-business sales involve merchandise that was brought in for the sale and labeled with fake discounts by a liquidator.

○ Look for online coupons by typing "coupon code" into a search engine.

* SHOES *

Women's Shoes

Women's shoes are far, far less expensive than they used to be, so much so that women can now buy a very fine pair of shoes for about $25. There's a tremendous variety and quality in that price range, so why pay more?

The lead character of the television comedy *Sex and the City*, Carrie Bradshaw, is crazy about shoes. She's always spending $400 on a pair of designer shoes. Of course the show is about the luxury lifestyle, with all four lead characters eating, drinking, and buying high-fashion clothes and wasting an incredible amount of money. In a very telling episode, Carrie almost loses her New York apartment because, while she has plenty of money to spend on shoes, she doesn't have enough, or good-enough credit, to buy her apartment when it goes co-op.

The reason shoes are so cheap today is that most are made overseas, where labor is far less expensive. Thirty years ago, almost all shoes sold here were made in the United States. Today, only 6 percent of shoes are made in the States. I'm in favor of free trade, so that's fine with me. But I recognize that some people are saddened by the decline of that business in the United States.

Just as consumers have moved away from department stores for many purchases, they have moved to specialty stores for shoes. There are expensive specialty stores like those in *Sex and the City*, but for the most part the specialty shoe stores are like the giant "category killer" stores that now dominate many other retail sectors. DSW, Designer Shoe Warehouse, is a well-known chain that sells a wide variety of excellent-quality shoes for about $25. A pair of Coach sandals that originally sold for $115 was recently on clearance at DSW for $28. Payless Shoe Source is another place to look, as is Target, which sells great shoes for as little as $12.

As prices drop, there's a risk of buying too many shoes. You may end up with 70 different pairs of black shoes, each a little different from another. If you reach the point where you can wear each pair only a couple of times a year, you probably have too many shoes.

Men's Shoes

Men rarely own more than ten pairs of shoes, and prices for those have dropped as well. I have three pairs of black loafers and I bought them at Costco for $15, $24, and $29. They don't sell them anymore. When I saw them go on clearance, I should have bought more.

One way to save on men's shoes is to look in the boys' department of the shoe store. Boys' shoes are almost always cheaper than men's shoes, even though the shoes may be exactly the same. That's because people won't pay as much for children's shoes. Children are so big now that many of the sizes overlap the adult sizes. Some kids wear size 15 shoes, bigger than almost any adult. I wear a size 11 and I've bought dress shoes and running shoes in the boys' department and saved about a third on the adult price. I bought a pair of brand-name Bass Weejuns in the boys' department for $34. Normally, they're $50 to $60 or more.

Men used to get their expensive dress shoes reheeled and resoled occasionally as they wore down. But shoes are so much cheaper, and shoe repair more expensive, that few people get shoes repaired any more. It usually doesn't make financial sense to get shoes fixed, especially men's shoes.

I wear running shoes far more often than dress shoes, because I like to run and I'm more comfortable wearing running shoes. Normally, I'm perfectly willing to accept lower quality for lower price. But I can't do that with running shoes. They have to fit comfortably and protect my feet and the rest of my body when I run. I learned that the hard way because I used to wear extra-cheap running shoes, and I injured myself because of them. The doctor put the blame squarely on those cheap shoes.

But I'm still able to save on running shoes. I buy very good quality shoes, but in last year's styles. If you think clothing is fashion-oriented, running-shoe wear is much worse. And prices gyrate wildly based on what's in and what isn't. So I buy all the misses—last year's hot color or the style nobody wanted. I'll usually pay $34 to $44 for very good running shoes. That's far less than the $200 some shoes now cost. A lot of guys have a closet full of fashionable athletic shoes. I benefit from being unfashionable.

You can find running shoes in sporting goods stores—although they're often overpriced—as well as warehouse clubs and discount stores. Outlet malls actually are a good place to score a deal on running shoes.

If you're not a runner, and you wear athletic shoes mostly to walk around in, the most important thing is to find a shoe that's comfortable. The price of those could be a whole lot less. Costco has its own brand of walking shoe that sells for as little as $12 to $15. My co-author, Mark Meltzer, certainly no shoe collector, likes to wear a pair of vintage white Converse All Stars he bought at Sports Authority for $25.

Kids' Shoes

Parents will do what they want, but I think you're crazy to spend a lot of money on kids' shoes. Their feet just grow too quickly. Children two to three years old will change sizes three times a year. School-age kids change sizes once a year.

Hand-me-down shoes make sense within a family, but you're probably not going to be excited about buying second-hand shoes for your children.

The best solution is buying shoes at Wal-Mart or Target, which have huge children's shoe departments and terrific prices. For a young child, you can get shoes for $3 to $8 a pair. As the kids get older, into school age, $13 to $18 is a good range.

I bought a pair of shoes for my younger daughter, Stephanie, for $5. They're good shoes, nicer than I would usually get, but they were marked down from $29 because they have a Pokémon logo on them and Pokémon isn't the red-hot phenomenon it was a few years ago. But what does she care? She's two and a half.

Parents sometimes worry that inexpensive shoes won't provide the proper support for a child's feet. But pediatrician Dr. Bob Kim says there isn't much to worry about, as long as your child's feet are normal to begin with. Children less than one year old don't need shoes at all, other than maybe to protect them from the cold when they're outdoors. For toddlers and pre-schoolers, there's no particular advantage to better-made shoes. When children reach school age and start playing soccer and other sports, all you have to do is look for athletic shoes that have a firm sole—rather than a spongy one—to provide proper support.

It helps to make sure your children's shoes fit right. The length should be about a half inch longer than the child's big toe and the width should allow you to pinch a little bit of the child's sneaker. The shoe should be snug enough to keep the heel from flopping up and down.

• Tips on Shoes •

○ Buy quality women's shoes for $25 or less at such stores as DSW, Designer Shoe Warehouse, Payless Shoe Source, and Target.

○ Save on men's shoes by looking in the boys' department of the shoe store.

○ Shoes are so cheap now that it usually doesn't make financial sense to get them fixed, especially men's shoes.

○ Save on running shoes by buying last year's hot color or the style nobody wanted.

○ For children, hand-me-down shoes make sense within a family. Or buy from Wal-Mart or Target, which have huge children's shoe departments and terrific prices.

✳ HAIRCUTS ✳

You can spend a lot of money getting your hair cut. But there are lots of ways to save.

Unless you have difficult-to-cut hair, there's no reason not to go to one of the chains that generally charge $10 to $15 for a haircut. They include Great Clips, Hair Cuttery, and Fantastic Sam's. Usually you get a great haircut, and it's not expensive.

If you go to a salon instead, you'll pay for the fancy environment rather than the haircut. Women have told me they've had terrible haircuts that cost $60 or more.

If you don't want to go to a chain, try to find a smaller place in your neighborhood. That probably will be cheaper than a big salon. Some salons also have training salons affiliated with them. They have people who have been hair-

cutters for years, but are training for a chair at the expensive salon.

Or look for salons that need models to try different hairstyles. For almost nothing, you can get a haircut for which others might pay $200. They're more likely to choose you if you are willing to accept a major change in your style, but they'll do a minor change as well.

Another alternative is a haircutting school. They have beginning haircutters who are being supervised by experienced cutters. They'll give you a good haircut at a great price.

I'd skip the school if you're looking for a cheaper way to get your hair colored. An inexperienced colorist can really mess up your hair. But you should be fine with a colorist who is training at one of the salon affiliates. The cheapest way is to use a store-bought hair color product, but the result is an all-one-color look that isn't as natural-looking as what a colorist can provide. If you're worried that it won't look good, try one of the semi-permanent products that wash out after three or four shampoos.

One of the simplest ways to save when you get your hair cut is to avoid buying the high-priced shampoos and other products they sell at the salon. That stuff is pure profit for the shop.

Nails

You don't have to go to a fancy spa to get a manicure and pedicure. Go to a national chain and it'll cost about $20 for your manicure and pedicure, which isn't bad. A lot of times it will include a neck and back massage, which feels great after a long week.

It's hard to do your own nails, but you can get your nails done for free if you're willing to do someone else's. Have a manicure-pedicure party with your book club or just a few friends, and you each do someone else's nails.

Or go to a school that trains people to do facials, skin treatments, manicures, and pedicures. You can get an amazing European facial that normally might cost $60 to $100 for just $30, or you can get cheaper facials. The students are supervised very carefully, and they all have to put in a certain number of work hours to get their degree. They need people to pamper.

Most nail salons don't heat-sterilize their manicure tools, so the best way to make sure you won't be harmed is to bring your own tools. That's especially true if you get your cuticles clipped.

Going to a school is the cheapest way to get a massage as well. Look in the phone book under cosmetology or massage schools, or search on the Web, and you'll get a deal.

* COSMETICS *

If you listen to the typical advertisement for women's cosmetics, you would think these products can do just about anything. The truth is, women waste a lot of money on over-hyped department-store creams that don't deliver what they promise.

In a January 2000 report, *Consumer Reports* found that a face lotion that cost $1.59 per ounce did a better job of moisturizing than a product that cost $32.35 per ounce. The bottom line is, you don't have to spend a lot of money to look beautiful.

You can buy most of the makeup products you might need for less than $50 at your local drugstore, says Karen Gerson Duncan, who has been a professional makeup artist for twenty-five years. That's $4 for mascara, $4 to $10 for lipstick, $5 to $10 for moisturizer with sunscreen, $8 to $12 for concealer cream and $10 to $13 for mattifier, an oil-reducing gel that Duncan loves. It's relatively new, but available from a number of manufacturers, including Neutrogena and Mary Kay. Add another $10 for blush, $8.95 for a set of four eye shadow colors, and another few bucks for an eyebrow pencil. Yet, many women will spend $250 or more at a department store cosmetics counter, trying to buy youthfulness that cosmetics can't deliver.

One of the most common claims in cosmetics ads, usually for a moisturizer, is that a product makes wrinkles less visible. One company claims its moisturizer "greatly diminishes the appearance of fine lines." Some products achieve this effect by using a mild irritant to puff up the skin around the wrinkles. But that's a temporary solution—it's not a good idea to constantly inflate and deflate the skin in this way, according to Duncan. Another product, if you can believe this, is a $350 department-store face cream that contains the foreskins of baby boys. It's hard to say which is more repulsive—the price or the ingredients.

If wrinkles are your chief complaint, see a dermatologist. A dermatologist can perform a technique called microdermabrasion, sometimes known as a "power peel" or a lunchtime peel, that essentially sandblasts away the top layer of skin and exposes the smoother layer of skin beneath. Or, a dermatologist can prescribe Retin-A, a medicine that strengthens skin and reduces wrinkles.

Duncan is not as fond of another popular medical solution, injections of the toxin Botox to paralyze muscles around the wrinkles. Duncan, who works with a variety of TV actresses, said casting directors are asking for women who have not used Botox, because the treatment lessens their facial expressiveness.

The main job of a moisturizer is to lubricate the skin with an emollient that replaces natural oils that aren't coming to the surface as they once did. That makes skin feel smoother and softer. Moisturizers use ingredients such as lanolin, glycerine, and mineral oil to do this. Most now add a sunscreen to protect skin from the wrinkle-inducing rays of the sun. You can't tell which moisturizer is better by the ingredients. According to *Consumer Reports*, "the top products all contain water and glycerin—but so do many others."

But you don't have to spend a ton of money to get a good moisturizer. You can buy a bottle of Oil of Olay lotion for about $8. Wal-Mart has a brand called Equate that does the same thing for even less.

Mascaras sell for $3.95 to $28.50, but all do the same thing, which is coat your eyelashes with a layer of waxy goop and dye to try and give your lashes the lush, full look they had when you were a child. People lose eyelashes as they age, and they get sparse. Duncan doesn't see any difference in quality among mascaras, so she recommends that you buy the most common, Maybelline. More important than the brand is to keep mascara only up to three months, after which the preservatives can no longer protect you from bacteria that could infect your eyes. Don't use anyone else's mascara, and don't let anyone in a department store put mascara on you, even if they use a new brush. It's unsanitary.

Duncan does see differences in quality among lipsticks. A more expensive lipstick does seem to last longer, and she will sometimes buy them at a department store. But again, for reasons of sanitation, don't test a lipstick on anything but your hand.

Duncan uses concealers to mask the circles-under-your-eyes effect that gets worse when people are tired or bothered by allergies. The circles come from blood flow beneath the skin, and it's more visible on some people than others. Duncan said she's had the best results with concealing creams that are yellow-based rather than green or purple. The products come in a stick or as a cream. She recommends creams because they don't dry as fast, and thus are easier to blend.

• Tips on Cosmetics •

❍ You can get a basic makeup kit together for less than $50 at your neighborhood drug store, including mascara ($4), lipstick ($4 to $10), moisturizer with sunscreen ($5 to $10), concealer cream ($8 to $12), and mattifier ($10 to $13).

❍ Don't rely on a moisturizer to fix wrinkles. See a dermatologist.

✳ EYEGLASSES AND CONTACT LENSES ✳

The amount of money people can spend on eyeglasses seems unlimited. I met a fellow in New York who spent more than $500 for a pair of glasses. It's not hard to find glasses at a much more reasonable price.

Consumer Reports has done several surveys of the eyeglass market, and has found consistently that people are the happiest when they buy their glasses from an optometrist in private practice, as opposed to an eyeglass chain. Unfortunately, that's one of the most expensive outlets for glasses.

Second in customer satisfaction is one of my favorite stores, Costco Wholesale. And next is a regional chain that's called For Eyes. Both Costco and For Eyes have the right mix of price, selection, and customer service.

I'm wearing a pair of Costco glasses now that cost $64 complete. The frames cost $39, and they're indestructible. For Eyes does a lot of two-for-one specials, so you can buy a pair of glasses and a pair of sunglasses for a good price, or a pair of regular glasses and a pair of computer or reading glasses.

If you can, wait until the Christmas holiday season, when no one else is looking to buy new eyeglasses, for specials. Check your Sunday newspaper for sale fliers.

Wherever you buy your glasses, stay away from the designer frames, or instead buy imitations of the designer frames. That's where the money can get away from you. You can buy good frames for as little as $19, and I'd consider up to $59 a reasonable price for frames. Sometimes you'll have to ask, "Where are your less-expensive frames?," because stores want you to buy the ones that cost $100 or more.

The disadvantage to buying at Costco or For Eyes is that you have to wait about a week for your glasses. That's not as convenient as the chains that will make your glasses in about an hour. But you pay a lot more for that convenience.

If you have vision insurance at your job, you might get an eye exam for free, but have to pay some charges for lenses and frames. And you might be restricted to buying at certain places. Even if you have insurance, you might end up paying more than you would without insurance at Costco or For Eyes.

There are a number of add-ons they'll ask you about when you buy glasses, and some make sense to buy. If you have weak eyesight and your glasses would be very thick, it makes sense to pay more for lighter and better-looking extra-thin lenses. A scratch-resistant coating makes sense for plastic lenses, which most people wear. I have to have anti-reflective coating because I wear my glasses on television. The anti-reflective coating is vulnerable to damage. They don't last nearly as long.

Contact Lenses

Contact lenses are a lot cheaper than they used to be. They've dropped by more than half in the last four years. So if you've considered contacts before but shied away because of the price, take another look.

You can buy contacts for less at a warehouse club, a discounter, or on the Internet. And they will be identical to the lenses you buy at your eye doctor's. They're exactly the same, so all you're doing is saving money. I found the best prices at Costco, just $13.95 for a box of Acuvue disposable contacts. But LensExpress (www.lensexpress.com) was cheaper than a retail store. When we

checked, they were selling for $18.95 a box, vs. $21.95 retail.

LensExpress also sells regular, non-disposable contacts, and you can order them at Costco. But regular lenses now represent a relatively small portion of the market.

You can save a ton of money, too, on contact lens solutions. You worry so much about the health of your eyes, and that fear might stop you from saving money by buying off-brand contact lens solutions. But as long as the ingredients are the same as the brand-name products you like, there's nothing to worry about. You have good eyesight because you're wearing lenses. Use it to compare ingredients on the label. If they're equivalent, buy the off-brand with confidence.

The savings are real. Costco's store-brand Kirkland Multi-purpose solution costs just 14 cents an ounce, and it had brand-name ReNu Multi-Purpose solution for just 42 cents an ounce, quite a bit cheaper than CVS's 69 cents an ounce.

• Tips on Eyeglasses and Contact Lenses •

❍ For great prices, buy your glasses at Costco Wholesale or the regional chain For Eyes.

❍ Stay away from designer frames, or look for imitations. You can buy great frames for $19 to $59. There's no need to spend more.

❍ Look for special deals during the Christmas holiday season.

❍ Buy contact lenses and solutions at Costco for the best prices. The lenses are identical to what the eye doctor sells. Solutions are equivalent. Just check the ingredients to see if they're the same as your brand.

• Internet •

www.lensexpress.com

✳ PRESCRIPTION DRUGS ✳

With prescription drug prices going through the roof, people have found a cost-saving alternative north of the border. Yes, Americans are buying their prescriptions, at much lower prices, in Canada.

People who live in cities such as Seattle, Detroit, and Buffalo can simply drive across the border and visit a Canadian pharmacy. But the rest of us can get the same discounts, from 30 to 70 percent off, online. One Web site, www.canadameds.com, has been so deluged with orders that it has had customer-service problems, including delays in shipping.

All you do is fax in your prescription and a few forms, plus your credit-card number, and your medicine arrives about two weeks later. The United States limits your supply to three months at a time, so you have to plan ahead. Obviously, this isn't a good idea if you need medicine for an emergency.

One of my listeners, Bill, was saving $2,800 a year by buying medicines for himself and his wife from Canada. He was buying arthritis medication for $27 instead of the usual $85, and his wife's cholesterol medicine for $67 instead of $141—for the same medication. It works because of Canadian price controls, and a good exchange rate between the Canadian and U.S. dollar.

It's completely legal, although controversial, because pharmaceutical companies and research hospitals believe that if consumers pay less for prescriptions, there'll be less money to fund research and development of new medicines. But the reality for many people is

that if they don't find a more affordable way to buy their medicines, they won't be able to buy them.

If you are sixty-five or older, or your parents are that age, you can take advantage of a number of discounts being offered by the drug companies. The offers are changing constantly, but there are two basic types. One is a cooperative effort from the industry to provide discounts to people who are over 65 and whose income doesn't exceed certain limits. Then there are programs from individual manufacturers, which are offering discounts only on medicines they make. With some programs you get a big discount; others let you pay a flat fee for your medicines, and still others provide them essentially for free. Since the offers are changing constantly, check my Web site, www.clarkhoward.com, for details.

The industry has adopted these programs because drug manufacturers are terrified that the federal government will impose price controls.

If you're not eligible for the discounts, you don't want to deal with

Canada, or if you need a prescription on short notice, it's time to visit your favorite warehouse club, because they have by far the lowest prices on prescriptions. We checked prices for the ten most-prescribed drugs and found Costco had the cheapest price on eight of them.

• The Ten Most-Prescribed Drugs •

(prices at Costco, CVS, and Walgreens):

1. **Hydrocodone w/APAP (10/500 tablet, quantity 60)**

   CVS—$31.09

   Walgreens—$30.99

   Costco—$39.39

2. **Lipitor (10 mg tablet, quantity 90)**

   CVS—$207.99

   Walgreens—$198.09

   Costco—$176.39

3. **Premarin (0.3 mg tablet, quantity 100)**

   CVS—$64.99

   Walgreens—$70.39

   Costco—$54.57

4. **Atenolol (100 mg tablet, quantity 100)**

   CVS—$27.19

   Walgreens—$23.99

   Costco—$16.37

5. **Synthroid (100 mcg tablet—quantity 100)**

   CVS—$45.09

   Walgreens—$44.99

   Costco—$31.29

6. **Zithromax (250 mg z pack tablet, quantity 6)**

   CVS—$49.39

   Walgreens—$49.99

   Costco—$42.49

7. **Furosemide (40 mg tablet, quantity 100)**

   CVS—$16.99

   Walgreens—$8.99

   Costco—$8.49

8. **Amoxicillin (500 mg capsule, quantity 30)**

   CVS—$14.59

   Walgreens—$13.99

   Costco—$8.17

9. **Norvasc (10 mg tablet, quantity 100)**

   CVS—$230.99

   Walgreens—$176.79

   Costco—$181.27

10. **Alprazolam (1 mg tablet, quantity 90)**

    CVS—$27.89

    Walgreens—$26.29

    Costco—$9.39

Wherever you buy, and whether or not you have health insurance that covers prescription drugs, you have to decide whether to buy generic or brand-name drugs. Many generics are exact pharmacological copies of brand-name drugs. Others are chemically different, but are supposed to treat the medical condition equally well. If the medicine is pharmacologically identical, you should have no problem choosing the generic, and saving money. If the generic isn't exactly the same as the brand-name, talk to your doctor about whether you should try it. And tell your doctor you may not be able to afford the brand-name drug.

About a third of all prescriptions are not filled at all because people can't afford them. The pharmacist will say, "That's eighty-two dollars," and the person will decide not to buy it. It makes more sense to try a generic than to not use any medicine at all.

Sometimes doctors will prescribe an expensive drug without realizing that another drug that would do just as good a job costs a lot less. The Internet now gives you the ability to compare different drugs and choose a cheaper alternative. You can check the drug your doctor prescribes at www.rxaminer.com, find a cheaper alternative, and see if your doctor will agree to prescribe the less-expensive drug. This is especially helpful with drugs you take regularly.

You can save on some medicines by getting a stronger dose and cutting the pills in half. Believe it or not, some medicines cost almost the same whether you buy, say, a 20-milligram or 40-milligram pill. So if you buy one hundred 40-milligram pills and cut them in half, you'll get two hundred 20-milligram doses for almost the same price. You'll cut your prescription prices almost in half.

Finally, you can lower your drug costs by using a plan your employer may offer called a cafeteria plan, or a flexible spending plan. You can use a flexible spending plan to help pay medical or child-care costs. You ask your employer to take a specified amount of money out of each paycheck, and you use that money to pay for medicines, deductibles, copayments, and other medical costs that aren't paid by the company health plan. The advantage is you can pay those costs out of gross, or before-tax, dollars. Since $200 off your gross pay often will equal $120 to $140 of your net pay, you get a substantial discount.

The downside is you can't tell your employer to take out more or less money during the year, and you lose any money that's left in the account at the end of the year. So if you have $1,000 taken out and draw only $600 from the account, you lose $400. That's the reason I generally don't favor using flexible spending accounts for medical care, except for known expenses like a prescription medicine. If you don't budget well, you can lose. However, because of the discount, you can lose a little money in the account and still come out ahead.

If you think you'll have $1,000 in prescription drug expenses in a year, try having $750 of your pay diverted to your flexible spending account. If you exceed the $750, pay the rest out of your net pay, and increase your contribution to the flexible spending account next year.

• Tips on Prescription Drugs •

- ○ Save by ordering your regular prescriptions online from Canada.

- ○ If you are 65 or older, or your parents are that age, check to see if the drug manufacturers offer senior discounts on the drugs you need.

- ○ If you need a prescription on short notice, buy from your local warehouse club for the best prices.

- ○ Check the drug your doctor prescribes at www.rxaminer.com, find a cheaper alternative, and see if your doctor will agree to prescribe the less-expensive drug.

- With some medicines, you can get a double-strength dose at a similar price and cut the pills in half.

- If you have access to a flexible spending plan at work, consider using that to pay your uninsured drug costs and copays with pretax dollars.

• Internet •

www.canadameds.com

www.rxaminer.com

✳ THE EMERGENCY ROOM ✳

The best way to save money on a visit to the emergency room is not to go. I'm not kidding.

In most large cities, you have the option of going to an emergency room or going to a "doc-in-the-box," those small medical offices where you can walk in without an appointment. Unless you have an extremely serious medical emergency, you'll do much better financially by going to a doc-in-the-box than an emergency room.

Emergency rooms are being swamped with patients, with maladies that range in severity from bumps and bruises to life-threatening injuries. As a result, the ERs are dysfunctional. Waits can be inordinately long and they're very expensive. If you have a cold and you're worried it might be something worse, you're far better off going to a doc-in-the-box. They're generally cheaper and you'll be seen faster. It's much less of a hassle.

Having said that, a visit to a doc-in-the-box may not be covered by your health plan, whereas visits to emergency rooms generally are covered, if you deem it to be an emergency. Under the law, if a reasonable person would consider it an emergency, you may go to the emergency room and get reimbursed for the care. You can figure out what to do by checking in advance to see how your health plan treats these kinds of situations.

I'm in an HMO, and it has a cooperative arrangement with some of the doc-in-the-boxes. So I pay the same amount for a visit there as I would to my HMO.

If your medical condition, or the medical condition of someone in your family, is truly serious, go to the emergency room. My co-author, Mark Meltzer, had to take his seventy-seven-year-old father, Morty, to the emergency room after a bad cold worsened. It was definitely the right call. Morty wound up spending two days in the hospital before he recovered.

If you do go to an emergency room, keep track of the bills you get and check to see what insurance pays and what you are responsible to pay. Don't ever assume a single bill is the entire bill. You may have separate bills for the attending physician, and for radiology. After thirty days, find out from the hospital if there is anybody else who needs to be paid, because you must submit a timely claim to your insurance company.

I hear often from people who are having trouble with their credit because they neglected to pay a bill following a visit to an emergency room. Often it's from a specialist or business allied with the emergency room (such as a radiologist or laboratory that might have done blood work) that might not have had your correct address. Ultimately, it ends up messing up your credit. So it's up to you, a month later, to figure out who you might owe, and file a proper insurance claim.

CHAPTER 4

LEISURE

My mother used to tell me, "All work and no play makes Clark a dull boy." I had so much ambition when I was younger that I never slowed down to enjoy things at all. But I've learned to take it easier. Now I take six weeks of vacation a year. During the other forty-six weeks I still work too much, but I do take time for myself.

While I believe in taking time for yourself, I also believe that spending too much money doesn't make your leisure time any more enjoyable. You can have a lot of leisure activity in your life, yet do it at a very reasonable cost. It's simply a matter of making minor changes, to spend less money. If you get a great bargain on a vacation trip, for example, you might save enough to pay for another trip. In this chapter, I'll tell you how to save money on books; music CDs; video games; movie, theater, and sports tickets; and vacations to ski or swim.

✳ MOVIES ✳

I was so disappointed by the demise of the dollar movie theater. But I soon realized that its passing was a good thing for movie lovers, because first-run movies are now coming out on DVD faster than ever.

People are buying DVD copies of movies—or watching films on pay-per-view—so soon after they first appear in the theater that second-run movie houses couldn't survive.

Some DVDs are now cheaper than music CDs. The movie studios have realized that they can sell a lot of DVDs by pricing them at less than twice the cost of a full-price theater ticket. Some less-popular movies can be had for less than $10. Popular movies are going for around $15 and major hits for $20. With a movie ticket going for $7.50 to $9 in most parts of the country, being able to buy a copy of a movie on DVD for $10, $15, or $20 is a good deal—especially if it's something you'll watch again and again. If you're not sure you're going to watch a movie more than once, you're better off renting it.

The cost to see a movie on pay-per-view or video-on-demand is even cheaper, about $3 for satellite and $4 for its inferior cousin, cable TV.

If you can't wait for the movie to come out on DVD or pay-per-view, you can save by time shifting: going to a matinee or twilight show for considerably less money. One theater chain near my home charges $7.50 for its evening shows, $5.50 for all shows before 4 P.M., and $3.75 for all shows that start between 4 P.M. and 6 P.M.

You also can save money on movie tickets by using discount coupons. One good source is the local coupon books, such as the Entertainment book. Search for a book online, and see if you like the coupon offers. You might be able to buy two movie tickets for the price of one at any AMC theater, or get one ticket for $5 at any General Cinema theater. But the coupons often aren't good for the first ten days to two weeks of a movie's run. Check newspaper ads, which may say, "No coupons accepted on this movie."

There's no harm in waiting a couple of weeks to see a new movie, and I think it makes more sense to do that. People who go the first weekend have bought into all the hype. People who go after the first couple of weeks are likely not only to get a better price, but to see a better movie, one that has received good word-of-mouth reviews rather than promotion.

The auto club, AAA, sells discount tickets to the major movie chains to its members. Discounts range from 50 cents to $2 off a full-price ticket. The movie chains also sell discount tickets on the Web, but only in packs of twenty or more tickets. They're aimed at corporations that want to give tickets to employees as incentives.

I'm a little embarrassed to say this, but I haven't been inside a movie theater in five years. It's funny, because I really enjoy movies, but we tend to watch them either on DVD or one of the pre-mium movie channels. We pay $11 a month and get six or seven channels of HBO, and there are other packages that combine several of the premium channels. If you love movies, paying $11 or so a month for a variety of movies is a good deal.

If you do see a movie in a theater, stay away from the concession counter. That's the place where movie theaters make most of their money, and you can lose much of yours. People have accused me of sneaking candy into theaters, which just about every theater prohibits. I can't remember doing that, but I don't buy refreshments in the theater. I just won't spend $3 on popcorn that costs the theater five cents, or $3 for a drink that I could buy at a convenience store for 59 cents. If you eat and drink before you go to the movie, the movie will cost a lot less. It's easy to imagine going to an evening movie and spending $18 on two tickets, and another $15 on popcorn and soda. Why pay $33 when you can enjoy the same movie for $7 to $10 and have lunch or dinner before or after? Or, for your $33, buy two DVDs or rent eleven movies on pay-per-view.

Another thing I don't do is rent movies from video rental stores, and I have a special dislike for the largest, Blockbuster Video. That's because of the huge number of complaints we get from people who use Blockbuster's "drop boxes" to return rented videos. Blockbuster makes an enormous amount of money on late fees. One out of every six dollars it takes in comes from late fees. Some of that just comes from customers not returning movies on time. Other times, it's the way Blockbuster processes videos that are returned. I saw this myself once, watching as a clerk told the guy in front of me that he owed $4 for returning a movie late. The customer said he had returned the movie on time, placing it into the store's drop box the night before the noon deadline. But the clerk insisted it was late, that it hadn't been clocked in until 1:30 P.M. The customer maintained, correctly, that it isn't his fault if the movie was returned on time but the store didn't get around to checking it in until after the deadline. Af-

ter considerable discussion, the manager waived the fee, but acted as if he was doing the customer a favor.

To avoid this kind of problem, don't use the honor system to return videos. Hand the video to a clerk and wait until he or she scans it in to record the return.

There's another way to rent movies that's a good deal and there are no late fees. With an online service called Netflix (www.netflix.com), you pay a monthly subscription fee of about $20 for basically all the movies you want to rent. When you sign up, you give Netflix a list of the movies you want to rent. They send you DVDs of the first few movies, and when you're done with one, you mail it back to Netflix in a postage-paid mailer they supply. Then they send you the next movie on your list. You can keep the movies as long as you want, with no late fees—your monthly fee is all you pay. If you're renting four or five DVDs a month, Netflix is a great alternative. Netflix made enough of an impression that Wal-Mart is launching an online service mimicking Netflix, at about a dollar less per month.

• Tips on Movies •

○ Going to an afternoon or twilight movie is considerably cheaper than going at night.

○ Check coupon books such as Entertainment for movie discounts. The auto club, AAA, also offers discounts to members.

○ Stay away from overpriced movie-theater concession counters.

○ A new service, Netflix (www.netflix.com), offers a much better alternative to renting DVDs from the local video store.

• Internet •

www.netflix.com   **(DVD rentals)**

www.ouraaa.com   **(Discount movie tickets from AAA)**

✳ MUSIC ✳

The outrageously high cost of music CDs actually has caused sales to decline. People are simply fed up. That a CD costs more in many cases than a feature film on DVD is inexcusable.

Now we know the reason. Five giant labels finally admitted that they had conspired to fix prices, setting a minimum price for each CD through a system called MAP. The good news is that CD prices are starting to fall, in some cases. I hope that leads to permanent price reductions.

Because the industry made CDs so expensive and failed to provide an online alternative, the free file-sharing service

Napster was born. Unfortunately, the industry defeated Napster in court and drove it out of business. The music industry, better late than never, also sells music for download. For example, you can purchase and download music at www.mtv.com, www.emusic.com, and www.cdnow.com.

If you can't find music on the Web, the best way around the high cost of CDs is to buy them used. If you go to a used-music store, you'll be able to listen to a CD before you buy it to make sure the sound is perfect, which it almost always will be. A CD isn't like an old vinyl record. If it's undamaged, the sound will be as good as the first time it was played. And prices are much cheaper. A store near me called Disc Go Round charges $5.99 to $8.99 for used CDs. I saw the Beatles *1* album, which retails for $18.98, on sale for $8.

People will often buy a CD because they think they like the artist, but then they find out that they don't, or they get tired of the CD. Those CDs go to the used-music store, waiting for you. And if you have old CDs you don't like, get some money for them by selling them to the used-music store near you. Disc Go Round, for example, pays $2 to $5 for your unwanted CDs.

Look for used-CD stores in alternative newspapers.

Another alternative is buying used CDs online. The Web site www.half.com offers two advantages: great prices and a wide selection that makes it more likely you'll be able to locate a hard-to-find CD, DVD, video game, videotape, or book. It's not an auction site, because there's no bidding. But you're buying from people, not a retailer. Sellers will tell you what condition the merchandise is in, and you buy with your credit card.

If you buy CDs new, you'll get the best prices at the warehouse clubs, but the selection will be limited to the hottest sellers. For a broader selection, try discounters such as Wal-Mart or electronics stores such as Best Buy or Circuit City. They often use CDs as a "loss leader," attracting customers with low prices to get them to buy equipment.

If you buy a lot of CDs, you might see a pattern in how retailers price them. Stores such as Wal-Mart and Best Buy often will market new titles with a sale price their first week out, or within the first four weeks. After six to eight weeks, they'll discount a title. After two or three months, it might go on clearance. If you can wait that long, you can pick up a new release for a few dollars less than its outrageous full price.

• Internet •

www.emusic.com
www.cdnow.com
www.half.com
www.mtv.com

* BOOKS *

The book business is going through a radical transformation as the independent shops steadily shrink and the chains that thought they could sell everything at full retail discover they can't.

There's no reason to pay retail anymore, because Amazon.com and the warehouse clubs are selling books for far less. In its most recent price experiment, Amazon began selling books priced at $15 or more at 30 percent off. Another online seller, Books-A-Million (www.bamm.com), allows you to join its online club for just $5 a year to get an extra 10 percent off all of its books. That's a great deal for people who love to read and love to save money. They'll even comparison shop for you. If their price isn't the cheapest, they'll show you who is cheaper.

Of course, online retailers can't offer you the ability to examine a book thoroughly. A great buy on a book you don't like is no buy at all. Chain and retail stores often offer great bargains, and always offer the opportunity to see and preview the books. You can also get great recommendations from knowledgeable staff. Another place to consider for books is an old standby, the local library, where you can still check out the books you love for free.

The warehouse clubs have really upset the applecart in the book business because, while they stock a very limited number of titles, they sell massive quantities of the books they choose to stock. They start with the *New York Times* bestsellers and discount them deeply, which has forced all the other booksellers to offer big discounts on those books. They also look for titles that they think will appeal to their cost-conscious customers.

Reference books, children's books, and cookbooks are huge sellers at the warehouse clubs. The savings on cookbooks are tremendous. Because the warehouse clubs sell groceries, they push cookbooks. After you look at the ingredients, you buy the groceries.

Another great way to save on books is to buy them used. Think of how many books people buy that they don't even read. I loved buying used textbooks in college, because the previous owner often underlined all the key things for me, so it was like having a set of Cliff's Notes.

One of the best ways to buy used is through a new chain called Half-Price Books, which sells used books at half their cover price. There are used-book stores in many cities, but they're usually kind of disheveled and poorly organized. Half-Price Books is professionalizing the sale of used books, and it's growing rapidly. As I write this, the company has locations in eleven states. You can find a location at its Web site, www.halfpricebooks.com.

• Internet •

www.amazon.com

www.bamm.com

www.halfpricebooks.com

✳ VIDEO GAMES ✳

As the price of high-tech video-game players drops, the biggest cost of playing is the game cartridges, which can run $50 to $80. So the secret to saving money is to buy games that were designed for the earlier generation of equipment, but still play perfectly on the new units. Stores that still sell PlayStation 1 games, for example, may price them at $8 or $14, a tremendous savings from the cost of the PlayStation 2 games. They won't have the same whiz-bang graphics, but they're fine. And that's probably going to be the case for the PlayStation 2 games if Sony comes out with a PlayStation 3. Generally no one wants the last generation of computer software. As soon as the new version comes out, demand for the old version dies.

You really stretch your dollar if you buy past-generation games. You might be able to buy four or five games for the cost of one new game. A good part of the fun for kids—and the kid in all of us—is being able to try different games. Instead, parents will blow $60 on a game for their son or daughter, and the kid will play that game until their eyeballs pop out. Then they're bored, and they want the next game. But parents can't always afford to drop $60 on a game. Instead, you could buy two PS1 games instead of one of the PS2. Or get one PS2 game and five PS1 games, instead of two PS2 games. You'll have to figure out what works in your family. But the savings are gigantic.

I went to one of the warehouse clubs

in Florida, and they had a giant display of PS1 games and the old Nintendo games. The bins were bursting with games, and they were incredibly cheap. I watched these boys, their minds shaped by advertising, walk right past them and go to a locked cabinet with the PS2 games. If these PS1 games were worth clamoring for a year ago, are they suddenly worthless? I don't think so.

Just make sure the old game will play on your equipment.

Another alternative is to buy the current games, but buy them used. Stores that sell video games often will take used games back as a trade-in toward new games, then resell the used ones at about half their original price. Wait a month or so after a new game is released, until people get burned out on it, and used copies of the game will start showing up at the video stores.

As far as the equipment goes, buy a new unit. The current generation of video-game players—the GameCube, the Xbox and the PlayStation 2—is phenomenal, and the cost of the machines is very reasonable. As I write this, the suggested retail prices are $149, $199, and $199. The PlayStation 2 was $400 at one point, so they've come way down in price.

One warning for parents: Some of the new-generation games, particularly the violent ones, are so realistic that you should read the box carefully. They have blood and guts that look like real blood and guts, like something you would see in an actual war. It's very graphic, and you might not want to buy it for your children.

✳ THEATER AND SPORTS TICKETS ✳

One of the best ways to save money on tickets is to do what I do—refuse to pay a junk fee to the monopoly ticket seller Ticketmaster. I won't buy tickets to an event through Ticketmaster under any circumstances.

Ticketmaster got its monopoly by going to arenas and concert venues and offering to pay for something the arena wanted. In exchange, it gained the exclusive right to sell tickets for the arena. Over the years, I've heard again and again from listeners about the poor service they've received from Ticketmaster. It makes the federal government seem like a customer-service-driven organization.

A listener named Dain Ferrero ordered a pair of tickets to a Robin Williams performance by phone through Ticketmaster, then got concerned when, three weeks later and just a couple of weeks before the show, he hadn't received his tickets. He called his local Ticketmaster office, and was treated rudely by a representative who said he was a manager. The manager offered to leave a replacement pair of tickets for Dain at the "will call" window, but Dain thought that was too risky. What if he went to the show and the tickets weren't there? Dain called the local office again and talked to a different manager, who was more cooperative. This manager told Dain what had happened—his tickets had been sent to the wrong address, an address that was not even remotely similar to Dain's. It was a

different street and ZIP code. The manager tried to be helpful, but he said the matter was out of his hands. He advised Dain to call Ticketmaster's corporate office in Orlando. When he did, the representative from the corporate office told Dain that tickets get sent to wrong addresses all the time. He deactivated the old tickets and sent Dain a new pair, which arrived in a few days. But it took three phone calls to clear up the mess.

Dain also had trouble when he bought tickets to a Billy Joel/Elton John concert through a Ticketmaster outlet in a local supermarket. Ticketmaster now uses a lottery system to prioritize ticket buyers, to discourage people from camping outside the store all night trying to be first in line. Unbelievably, Ticketmaster's store representatives told prospective customers that if they took a lottery number, then didn't buy tickets, they would call the police. I'd love to know what the charge would have been. The store reps also advised customers that they would be pulling the $200 seats first, then the $140 seats, then the $90 seats. They said customers who drew low lottery numbers would have to buy the $200 seats, even if they wanted cheaper seats. Dain and his wife drew a low number and had to buy the $200 seats, even though they wanted the $140 seats. When they called Ticketmaster to complain, Ticketmaster blamed the errors on the supermarket representatives, who they said were poorly trained. The tickets turned out to be very good, so Dain and his wife decided to keep them.

You can avoid these kinds of hassles by buying tickets from the venue's box office, if the box office sells tickets directly. That's what I do. Buying directly saves me the Ticketmaster fee and the potential hassle of dealing with an organization that doesn't care about its customers.

Many cities now have discount ticket booths, modeled after the famous TKTS half-price ticket booths in New York City's theater district. Like TKTS, these booths offer half-price tickets on the day of the performance for cultural events, concerts, the symphony, and plays. You may not be able to get tickets for the event you most want to see, but you'll save a lot of money, and if you're really into theater, you'll get to see a lot more theater for a lot less money.

Another way to save on movies, theater, and other kinds of entertainment is to use the Entertainment coupon book. It's available around the country, but has different discounts in each city. Before you buy it, check www.entertainment.com to see what discounts are included in your local book.

I save money on sports events by going to the stadium without a ticket and buying at the last minute. At a football game, for example, I might have to wait until kickoff. Once the game begins, whether it's the tipoff in basketball, the first pitch of a baseball game or the face-off in hockey, any tickets that remain become spoiled goods. I find that I can buy tickets outside the event, even for a team that's a contender, for 25 to 50 percent of the face value of the ticket. It doesn't work for a narrow number of events—a championship game or playoff game for which the demand is overwhelming. I avoid the professional ticket sellers, because then you pay a middleman's markup. Instead, I go to where the season ticket holders park, and where they walk to the stadium, and I hold up a few fingers representing how many tickets I need. That's illegal in some places, but it's usually legal— even in places where scalping is illegal— as long as you're paying less than the face value of the ticket. When you buy direct from a season ticket holder, usually a corporate type, they're stuck with the ticket and they're happy to get anything for it.

Last season I took my daughter to a pro football game and we paid $5 a ticket for tickets on the 40-yard line that had a face value of $38. That's a good score. The downside is that you have to be willing to go home and not see the game. That happened to me once. There was a big walk-up crowd for a game, and I couldn't find a deal on tickets. So I went home.

Another option is to take the family to a minor-league game, for which tick-ets are far less expensive. Because big-league sports have priced their tickets out of the reach of some ordinary fans, minor-league teams, with their low pay-rolls and overhead, are finding they can operate right near big-league teams.

A lot of the big-league baseball, bas-ketball, and hockey teams sell a small number of seats at reasonable prices, maybe $5 or $10. Check with your local teams to see. It doesn't have to cost you $282 to take a family of four to a game. Eat beforehand rather than at the ball-park and buy the bargain seats. My daughter Rebecca still talks about the time I took her to a hockey game years ago and sat in the $10 seats. There were all these drunk people around, and they made a big impression. It's a different crowd up there than down below.

With concerts, there's no way to get a good deal if you want to see a singer or a group that's hot. Music fans will wait on long lines to get tickets, and pay outrageous prices and ticket sur-charges. When you're dealing with something that involves a fanatical desire, the choice you make is that price doesn't matter. Before my wife, Lane, met me, she and a friend wanted to go to a concert at an open-air amphitheater, and they couldn't afford the tickets. They went there and couldn't find any bargain tickets, but he had a convertible, so they just drove around and around the amphitheater, listening to the show. You can't sit still, because the police make you move along. So they just circled.

• Tips on Tickets •

❍ Go to the box office for your tickets and don't pay the outrageous fees to Ticketmaster.

❍ Many cities now have discount ticket booths, modeled after the famous TKTS half-price ticket booths in New York City's theater district.

❍ For sports events, try going to the stadium on game day and buying tickets from season ticket holders who have extras. It's usually legal as long as you pay face value or less.

❍ Another option is to take the family to a minor-league game, for which tickets are far less expensive.

• Internet •

www.entertainment.com

Skiing is an ultra-white-collar sport, but you don't have to pay ultra-high prices to enjoy it. I have some great tips that will save you money on ski equipment, clothing, and lift tickets. If you prefer the beach to the ski mountains for your vacation, I'll save you some money there, too.

The biggest mistake people make when they go on a snow skiing vacation is to buy their clothing in their hometown. If you live in a part of the country that doesn't have ski mountains and you buy your ski stuff at local stores, you'll pay a fortune. In these "fly-out" markets, you'll have only ultra-high-end retailers selling ski clothing and equipment.

The far better deal is to buy what you need when you get to your ski destination, whether it's Colorado, Utah, parts of New England, Washington, or Oregon. At these "fly-in" markets, you can go to places like Wal-Mart and buy ski bibs (a one-piece snowsuit) for $15.99, instead of the $200 to $400 a pair you'll pay at high-end ski shops in fly-out markets. You can buy ski socks, thermal underwear—whatever you need—very inexpensively, in communities near the ski mountains. But don't buy at the resort. That's important. All the bibs I have come from Sam's Club, Kmart or Wal-Mart. Obviously, the ones I buy don't have the cutest little designs and the latest fabrics. They just make you comfortable when you ski. If you want to look like one of the "ski bunny" crowd, you'll have to pay a lot more than I do.

The best way to save on equipment is to buy it used. There are a lot of people who got into skiing and maybe got hurt or got too old to want to ski anymore—or maybe just decided they didn't like it, but had already spent a lot of money on equipment. That's created a huge used market in skis, boots, and poles, and you can buy the equipment at deep, deep, deep discounts. We bought Lane's skis for $49. Brand-new, they would have cost about $600. And they had very little use on them.

I got my skis new for $49 at an end-of-season sale. It was a line of skis in a bland gray color, with a red stripe, that people didn't like. I don't care what color they are. Those kinds of sales are very common in ski areas, especially in larger cities near ski towns such as Denver and Colorado Springs, Colorado, Salt Lake City, Utah, and Portland, Oregon. In cities like those, where people drive to nearby resorts, skiers don't have a lot of money, but want to ski. Used equipment sales also are an annual event in the ski cities and on the West Coast, usually in August or around Labor Day. San Diego has one every year. They're like giant flea markets.

The rising popularity of snowboarding also has increased the supply and depressed the prices of ski equipment. People who have switched to snowboarding are getting rid of their ski equipment.

To save on lift tickets, ask locals where they get their discount tickets, because only the fly-in market pays full price for lift tickets. Locals buy them at supermarkets, drugstores, and restaurants that offer discounts on lift tickets as an incentive to shop there. Ski cities also have what are known as "locals' mountains," which don't have a lot of fancy resort housing and cater to people from the region who drive in for a day of skiing. They're good mountains, but aren't really known to outsiders, who are known in ski lingo as "Flatlanders." You can get a much lower price-per-day skiing at a locals' mountain than at a fly-in mountain. In the Denver area, for example, locals might go to Winter Park, while Flatlanders go to Breckenridge.

If you're learning to ski, locals' mountains have far cheaper prices on "learn-to-ski" packages, which combine equipment, lift ticket, and lessons. These packages can cost as little as one quarter the cost at a locals' mountain, where they hope to get you back again and again, than a fly-in mountain, where they know the revenue is coming in just once.

Golf

You can save a lot of money by buying your ski equipment used, and you can do the same if you decide to try golf. Golf frustrates people to death, so there's a huge supply of used clubs from all those people who tried the game and quit. There's also very little demand for used clubs, because golf is such a country-club sport that most golfers wouldn't consider buying used clubs. With plenty of supply and little demand, the price of used clubs is very low. We checked a used sporting goods store called Play it Again Sports, which sells golf clubs for as little as $1 a club up to $600 for a set of very fancy clubs. It had a top-of-the-line set of Mizuno T-Zoid irons, which normally sell for $699 to $799, for $300, and the clubs looked brand new. There were good sets of irons for $150 and beginner sets for less than $100.

If you're an experienced golfer, look for used golf clubs on eBay (www.ebay. com), a store that specializes in used sporting goods, or in the classified ads of your local newspaper. If you're thinking of trying golf, ask an experienced golfer to help you.

The Beach

One of the best ways to save on a summer beach vacation is to go in June instead of July or August. Parents tend to schedule activities for their children, such as summer camps, to begin right after school ends. That pushes family vacations back to the end of summer, and this phenomenon has created an end-of-summer spike in demand that has affected everything from weekly beach rentals to travel to Europe. June, which used to be the heart of beach vacation season, has become more like a spring month at many beach locations. Because demand is less in June, there's a great opportunity to save money on accommodations.

If you're interested in going to a Florida beach, those in South Florida, particularly on the Gulf Coast, are much cheaper in the summer than are North

Florida beaches. South Florida beaches have their peak season in winter, when North Florida is too cold. In the summer, when you're most likely to want to go to the beach, South Florida is in its off-season.

The ultimate bargain time for the beach is in September, when kids are back in school. So if you don't have children or your kids are grown or preschool age, that's a great time to save. There are no customers at that time for beach accommodations and the weather is still warm, even in North Florida.

As you consider rental properties, check their rate cards for the seasonal cutoff dates. In many cases you can save big by planning your vacation for the period just after rates dip. Sometimes you can save even during a busy time, by staying in a hotel or rental property that caters to conventions and conferences but that doesn't have any big meetings booked for that time. Computerized systems now automatically adjust prices based on demand. So if demand dips, prices immediately fall.

Another factor is the booming second-home market. Lots of aging baby boomers have bought second homes, which they rent out when they're not vacationing. That's created a supply of rental homes much greater than the demand to rent them, both at the beach and the mountains. A good way to take advantage of that is by renting through a real-estate agency rather than a resort property manager. Whether you rent a house or a condo, you won't get the same frills, such as nightly maid service, or consistent quality. One house or condo may be beautifully decorated, while another may be sparsely decorated or even dumpy. So you'll want to see interior pictures of the unit you want to rent, and they're often available on the Internet. But you'll pay much less. A weekly rental through a real-estate agency might cost half what a similar rental would through a resort operator. A monthly rental through a real-estate agency might cost only twice what one week costs. So you get four weeks for the cost of two. In the summer of 2001, I rented an oceanfront three-bedroom condo for a month for $3,100, or $100 a day. The property, when rented through a resort operator, costs $450 a night, with a minimum of three nights. I needed it for only three weeks, but it was much cheaper for me to rent it for a month than it would have been for me to go through the resort operator.

You can score even better deals, but with even less service, by dealing directly with the owner rather than a resort operator or a real-estate agency. During the summer of 2000, I rented an efficiency on the ocean for a month for $1,000, or a little more than thirty dollars a night. There was no maid service for the entire month, but washing your own sheets and towels is a small price to pay for that kind of savings.

You can find real-estate agencies and individual property owners online by typing in the city and the phrase "beach rentals" at your favorite search engine. This works well in Florida and also in Hawaii.

Accommodations are the primary cost of a beach vacation, because most people drive to the beach rather than fly. If you're already on the road, it may make sense for some travelers to consider driving another few hours to South Florida rather than North Florida. You could cut the cost of your vacation in half. On the Gulf Coast of Florida, look from Clearwater to Marco Island. On the Atlantic Coast of Florida, look from Melbourne Beach down to Miami.

Florida, which has some of the world's best beaches, is a good choice even for people in the Northeast United States or in California. Southern Californians can fly to South Florida, and pay for their airfare and accommodations, for about the same amount as a beach resort in nearby Laguna. And they won't have to deal with the crowds. For people in the Northeast, why pay a fortune for a rental on a crowded beach on Long Island or Nantucket? Get a bargain airfare and fly to Florida.

Prices in the Caribbean are lower in

the summer also, but they're still very expensive.

There are other costs to a beach vacation, and other ways to save. People look at me as if I've lost my mind on some things, but here's what I do: It's much cheaper to buy your own beach chairs at a discount store and take them with you to the beach than it is to rent a beach chair. Sunscreen is a lot cheaper at Wal-Mart than at the beach, and so are beach towels. Take a trip to your neighborhood dollar store and see what you find there. My co-author, Mark Meltzer, picked up some name-brand children's sunscreen for $1, along with a number of pool and beach toys.

Sunglasses are a good item to buy at the dollar store as well. People think they need to spend a lot of money to protect their eyes from the sun, but it isn't true. All sunglasses are required to meet certain standards for sun protection, and they do. We bought four pairs of sunglasses for $9, $19, $49, and $109, and had them all tested at a lab.

All four blocked at least 90 percent of ultraviolet rays. In fact, the $9 pair blocked the most UV radiation.

When you pay more for sunglasses, you're paying for styling.

Amusement Parks

Both the regional and national amusement parks offer season passes that allow unlimited visits for people who live in the area. Or you can buy a less-expensive pass that's good for certain times of the year. If you think you'll visit the amusement park two or more times, it makes sense to buy one of these locals' passes.

In Florida, there's the Florida Residents Pass for Disney, and Universal Studios has one as well. But don't think you're going to be able to call your long-lost cousin who lives in Florida or California and have them buy a pass for you. The attractions prevent that by making you show a local driver's license. You might be able to do it for a child. Many parks also offer a second day free, or a discounted second day if you purchase admission at the same time you buy the first day. If you think you might want to go back a second day, ask what a second-day pass costs. It's worth a gamble even if you're not sure, because the price is great. The parks make their money on concessions and parking.

Another way to buy discounted amusement park tickets is through AAA, the auto club (www.ourAAA.com). AAA sells tickets to its members for several dollars off the regular price of many attractions.

Be very mindful of all the signs you'll see, especially in Orlando, that promise free or extra-cheap tickets to an amusement park. To get them, you'll have to go to a time-share presentation, and as I detailed in my previous book, *Get Clark Smart*, time-shares are a terrible rip-off. If you think the tickets are worth the time you'll give up, and if you know yourself well enough to know that you won't buy a time-share no matter how enticing they make it seem, go ahead and do it. I had a caller who went to three time-share presentations while in Orlando. He and his wife got into Sea World and Universal Studios for free, and got into Disney World for just $20 a ticket. They would schedule their day by going to time-share presentations in the morning and the amusement parks in the afternoon. It makes sense if you can go with the flow like that because the tickets cost a fortune—usually $200 per day for a family of four, just to get in the door. That's big money. The people who sell the time-shares know some people will try to take them for the tickets. But they also know they'll get enough buyers to easily cover the cost of the tickets.

I did a hidden-camera visit to a time-share presentation in Orlando, and the salesperson knew right away that there wasn't anything he could say to get us to buy. So he chatted with us for a while, told a supervisor it was hopeless, and let us go early.

• Tips on Vacations •

o Buy your ski equipment, clothing, and lift tickets in the ski town you're visiting, not in the city where you live. But don't buy at the ski resort.

o Consider buying used ski equipment.

o Ask locals where they buy their discount lift tickets.

o Visit locals' mountains rather than resorts that cater to fly-ins.

o Plan your summer beach vacation for June, instead of July or August. Better yet, if you don't have children in school, go in September.

o Beaches in South Florida, particularly on the Gulf Coast, are cheaper in the summer than those in North Florida.

o Rent from a real-estate agency or a property owner rather than a resort property manager, for big savings.

o Buy beach chairs and sunscreen at your local Wal-Mart rather than at the beach.

o Consider a second-day ticket for an amusement park if you think you might visit a second time during your vacation.

o Beware of offers you'll see, especially in Orlando, that promise free or extra-cheap tickets to an amusement park. To get the tickets, you'll have to go to a time-share presentation, and time-shares are a terrible rip-off.

CHAPTER 5

ELECTRONICS
+APPLIANCES

Americans spend a lot of money on electronics and appliances, and it's amazing that we often make these purchases with virtually no information, or with information that comes straight from a salesperson. I would rather you step back, follow a few simple steps, and make smart buying decisions that will be good for your wallet and bring you enjoyment.

With electronics, we frequently overpay for what we need. We're too willing to pay more for a few bells and whistles we'll probably never use. That's even more likely if you're listening to salespeople, who sometimes get extra under-the-table money known as "spiff" to steer you to a particular item. The choices in these stores are so confusing that shoppers have a tendency to come in intending to buy one thing and leave with something else.

Do your homework up front and figure out what you want to buy. Unless you discover an overwhelming reason why you were wrong, stick with what you intended to buy.

In this section, you'll learn how to do that research, enjoy your purchase, and not overpay.

✳ CONSUMER ELECTRONICS ✳

People are going to the movies less and watching movies at home more, and one of the ways they're doing that is in a home theater. Everyone is looking to duplicate the incredible sound you hear in the movie theater.

A friend of mine spent $70,000 custom designing and remodeling a room in his house as a home theater, and that's not at all unusual. People are routinely spending $50,000 or more to build and equip home theaters.

My friend's home theater was incredibly impressive. The screen could be lowered and raised at the push of a button. The audio and video equipment was housed in beautiful built-in cabinets. It was really neat. But you pay an awful lot for the consultants who come into your home, draw all kinds of sketches, and write formal proposals to

craft a system with just the right brands and equipment.

My wife, Lane, and I put in a home theater, and as you might guess, we did it for considerably less than $70,000. We took a storage room in our basement that we didn't really need for storage and installed new drywall and carpet. Then we equipped it with off-the-shelf rather than custom components. You can buy a "theater-in-a-box," which contains the entire sound system, including the speakers and the amplifier, and functions as the nerve center for a home theater system. Other components, such as a DVD player, TV, and VCR, plug into the amplifier, like the receiver on a music system.

We bought a theater-in-a-box, a 60-inch television, a DVD player that holds five discs, and a stereo VCR—all for about

$2,500. That didn't include the cost of carpeting or drywall.

Most people start with the TV, but you should start with the sound system. Don't worry about the technical specifications. Just listen to how it sounds in the store. Most people won't be able to discern differences in quality between a good, modestly priced system and a super-expensive one.

You do have to be mindful of the room. A den usually works best. Most movie theaters are rectangular, because that's best for the acoustics. It would be hard to create a home theater in a very open room.

People watch a movie in our home theater and they can't get up, because the sound and the picture are just so fantastic. I get such a kick out of the fact that we spent tens of thousands of dollars less than my friend. I'm sure his is 10 percent better, but it's not 30 times better. More important, a lot of people can afford to spend a few thousand dollars to set up a home theater but could not afford to spend $50,000 to $70,000. You can have a fantastic audio-video system in your home without spending a fortune.

If you really want to duplicate the movie experience, consider spending another $200 for a device called a Butt Kicker. It responds to the bass by shaking the floor.

DVD Players

People tend to overpay for their home-theater components, and there's really no need to do so. We have a five-disc DVD player that cost $129, so we can be true couch potatoes and watch five movies in a row without changing discs. I saw a three-CD changer for $99.99. But you can buy a single-disc DVD player for about $60 that will give you a terrific picture and sound. You won't get a better picture if you spend more. If a $60 DVD player breaks, you just throw it away and get a new one. But with most consumer electronics, problems either will be evident right away, or it will work beautifully for years.

If you have a high-definition television, you need a DVD player that has progressive scan, which will give you a higher-quality picture.

If you think the DVD caught on fast, you're right. The DVD player is the most successful home entertainment device in history, according to Warren Lieberfarb, president of Warner Home Video. It went from zero to 30 million households in its first five years, faster than CDs, VCRs, home computers—even faster than the television itself.

VCRs

Some stores aren't even renting video-cassettes any more, but it still makes sense to have one in your system. Even if you have a DVD player to watch movies, you'll need a VCR to record programs (unless you use a personal video recorder to do that) and play your old tapes. Recordable DVD units will offer another option for recording, as soon as the price comes down to reasonable levels.

You can get a very fine, four-head, stereo VCR for about $60, maybe less.

TVs

Listeners keep asking me about them, but as I write this, high-definition televisions still aren't ready for most of us to buy. Nobody is transmitting programming that works for it, and the broadcasters and the government are still arguing over standards for transmission and reception of high-definition television. Back in 1996, the government set a deadline requiring all television be transmitted in digital form by 2006, which has since been extended to 2007. I wouldn't be surprised if the United States doesn't go all-digital until 2017.

The result is that people who are buying high-definition television today may end up with something that turns out to be an interim technology, something that ultimately is not how people watch television. The standards fight, which is worse than the 1980s fight over videocassette recorder technology, will go on so long that a succeeding technology may take its place.

Most high-definition TVs sold today

are really "high-definition ready," which means they come without a high-definition tuner. Even if you spend $1,500 for the TV, you're still going to have to spend another $700 or $800 on whatever tuner the industry decides will be the standard. The picture in the store may take your breath away, but it doesn't make sense yet to buy a high-definition TV.

That leaves two other categories of television. Traditional analog TVs continue to fall in price. As I write this, you can buy a 36-inch stereo TV for $549, a 32-inch TV for $329, a 27-inch TV for $220, or a 19-inch TV for less than $100. That's incredible.

Flat-screen TVs provide another alternative. They have a crisper, clearer picture than traditional TVs, but they're much cheaper than the not-ready-for-prime-time high-definition TVs. Flat screens once were three times the price of a traditional TV. Now they're 33 percent to 50 percent more. You'll have to decide whether you want to spend more for a better picture. Or you can get a traditional 27-inch for the same price as a flat-screen 20-inch TV. I like a bigger screen and a cheap price, so I'm still buying traditional TVs.

If you want a giant-size TV, larger than 36 inches, those are sold almost exclusively in high-definition models.

As far as features, almost all TVs now have stereo sound. You can pay extra for picture-in-picture, but people with satellite TV, like me, can't use PIP. For what you pay extra for a PIP TV, you could put a $100 19-inch TV next to your main TV and have a better picture on the second screen. I went to a guy's house who had gone a step beyond that. He had a big-screen TV surrounded by six smaller TVs in his media room. TVs are so cheap now that some people can afford that.

Don't ever buy service contracts for your electronics. With prices this cheap, if something breaks you just replace it. I bought a TV for $199, and when the manufacturer's warranty ended, I got a letter from the electronics store trying to get me to buy a five-year extended warranty on the TV. The cost of the warranty was $249—more than I paid for the TV.

Digital Cameras

Like most new consumer electronics items, digital cameras were very expensive when they first came out. But now they're remarkably affordable. For $200 or less, you can get a quality digital camera that will do everything you want it to. Look for a camera with a resolution of 2.1 megapixels, the level of picture clarity that's fine for most uses. A professional photographer might need a higher resolution than that, but unless you're a pro, you won't.

What's really important with a digital camera is how easy it is to use. A lot of digital cameras end up collecting dust on the shelf because people get too frustrated with the owner's manual to use them. Get a camera that a child could pick up and use.

Third, your camera should make it easy to transfer your pictures to a computer to store or print. I've had one for six months, but I've yet to print a picture because I can't figure out how. That's not good. The ones that people find easiest to use have a docking station that you connect to a port on your computer. Then, when you come home with your camera, you put it into the docking station and the pictures come right up on your screen. You can print them or attach them to an e-mail. The docking station is similar to the ones people use with Palm Pilots or other handheld computers. Some cameras link directly to a printer.

Memory is a "gotcha" with some digital cameras. Some come with very little memory, and buying additional memory can cost as much as the camera. My brother-in-law spent $400 on additional memory. You want a camera that will store—at the highest resolution—the equivalent of eight rolls of film, or about 200 pictures. When you get home from a trip, you can download the pictures to your computer. One thing that's great about digital cameras is you don't have to keep pictures you don't like. Sometimes, with film, you'll shoot two or three pictures just to make sure you get one you like. With a digital camera, you can look at the image right away. If somebody closed their eyes or a car drove by and ruined the shot, you can just delete it and take another. You don't have to shoot as many images as you would with a film camera.

Camcorders

Unless you want to share videotapes with other family members, it doesn't really matter what type of video camera you buy. Price is the main factor, and you can buy a good one now, very nicely featured, for $200 to $250.

Video cameras have shrunk dramatically in size over the years, because people don't take big cameras with them. If you like to travel and don't like to lug a lot of stuff with you, it's worth paying more for a smaller camera.

Most people buy a video camera after the birth of a child, and if your main purpose is to shoot video of your child at home, any camera will do. They all provide good pictures.

There are a few basic formats for video cameras. There are two basic analog types. VHS C uses tapes that drop into an adapter, which then pops into your VCR. Hi8 uses 8-millimeter tapes.

There are several types of digital camcorders, including the super-small MiniDV camcorders, and Digital 8, which gives digital quality on Hi8 tapes. There's also a new generation of disc-based digital camcorders. Some use DVD-R, which are compatible with DVD players but can be recorded on only once. Others use DVD-RAM, which can be recorded on again and again, but are not compatible with DVD players.

Digital cameras offer better picture quality and they allow you to transfer video to your computer. If your relatives have high-speed Internet access, you can e-mail video to them. But if they have regular dial-up Internet access, forget about doing that. Downloading the video would take hours.

Digital camcorders are still considerably more expensive than analog, so unless you plan to e-mail or edit video, which few people do, I'd stick with analog.

Personal Video Recorders

I love personal video recorders, which allow you to record television shows and movies onto a computer hard drive rather than videotape, at the same level of quality as the original program. We have one called ReplayTV, made by a company called SONICblue Inc. TiVo is the major player in the marketplace, and there are several private-label recorders.

What makes PVRs so neat is they do the thinking for you. You tell it what kind of shows you're interested in, and it does the rest. Let's say you love M*A*S*H, which is on at all different times of the day or night on many different channels. You just tell the PVR you like M*A*S*H and it finds the episodes and records them. Let's say you're a Tom Cruise fan. You tell that to the PVR and it will record anything Tom Cruise is in.

PVRs also allow you to pause a live TV show, say to answer a phone call, then resume watching the show when you want. With a VCR, you would have to wait until the show is over, then rewind the tape and watch from the point you began recording and answered the phone. A PVR will let you resume watching at any time, even as it continues to record the end of the program. They're really remarkable.

PVRs also allow you to skip commercials more easily than a VCR, and that's landed the manufacturers in court. As I write this, there's been no resolution.

Lane and I took my mom to dinner during the Super Bowl—that's a great time to go because restaurants aren't crowded—and we recorded the game on ReplayTV. We got home two hours after kickoff, and then I started watching the game from the beginning. Some people enjoy the commercials during the Super Bowl as much as the game, but I just skipped through them. I also skipped the halftime show. And I caught up with the game—after starting two hours late—late in the third quarter.

People who have PVRs just about worship them. They consider them a mandatory appliance—something they wouldn't do without. That says a lot.

The difference among PVRs isn't features. It's the monthly or lifetime programming fee and how many hours of programming it can store. With most PVRs, you pay a monthly fee of $5 to $13, or a one-time fee of perhaps $250. Over time, it's cheaper to pay the one-time fee. The danger with this, or any up-front fee, is that the company could go bust. We've had our ReplayTV for three years, so paying the one-time fee worked out well. But we really didn't have an option. At the time we bought it, the one-time fee was included in the cost of the unit.

You can buy PVRs that can hold 30, 40, 60, or 80 or more hours of programs. We have a 60-hour machine, and it's plenty of capacity. Our first machine was a 20-hour machine, and that wasn't enough, but with 60 hours we've never had a problem. Lane can record every episode of every different *Star Trek* series—*Next Generation, Deep Space Nine,*

Voyager, and *Enterprise.* She doesn't like the original series.

Some manufacturers are combining PVRs with other devices, such as DVDs, and that may help broaden their appeal.

To use a PVR, you may have to have a phone line accessible. During the night, PVRs dial into the company's system and download and update the programming guide for the next two weeks. If the World Series plays a sixth game, it loads that information into its system.

One danger of buying a PVR is that, unlike with a VCR, you need the services of the company that sells the device. If the company goes out of business, like a lot of technology companies have, your machine could become an expensive paperweight. The technology could be acquired by another company even if the original company fails, but it's still a risk. Other than a cell phone, there isn't another device that works only with one company. The satellite TV companies deal with this by renting the service rather than making you buy the equipment.

✳ LARGE APPLIANCES ✳

When you bought your last refrigerator, dishwasher, or washer and dryer, you probably based your decision on the brand name of the appliance, its features, and price, in whatever order was most important to you. Now I'd like you to add a fourth criterion—energy usage.

Your refrigerator is one of the biggest energy users in your house. So when it's time to buy a new one, it might be worthwhile to spend a bit more up front to buy a refrigerator that will use less electricity each year.

Large appliances now carry an Energy Star label indicating they are rated for low energy usage by the federal government, or rated for low water usage for products such as dishwashers and clothes washers. That label generally means you'll save a fortune in operating costs through the years.

When I bought a dishwasher several years ago, I chose an Energy Star dishwasher even though, at the time, Energy Star dishwashers cost a lot of money. Making dishwashers energy efficient, and efficient in their use of water, was new technology at the time, so these appliances cost a lot more. But the Energy Star dishwasher I bought recently was just $239 on sale at Home Depot. That's the same or less than what people typically would pay for a dishwasher—and it does a great job of cleaning the dishes. If an Energy Star appliance costs the same as the one that uses more energy and/or water, it's an easy decision.

If the Energy Star appliance costs more, it may or may not be worthwhile to buy it. I recently had to replace a refrigerator/freezer, and I bought a 25-cubic-foot model with icemaker for $799. The cheapest Energy Star model I could find of the same size was $1,249. So I checked the estimated energy usage on the labels, and the Energy Star refrigerator was projected to use only $5 less electricity per year. So I would have to live to be 840 years old (137 really) to make that pay off. In that case I made the decision to buy the much cheaper refrigerator and pay $5 extra a year for electricity. That was a rare case. Very likely, the refrigerator I bought was right on the cusp of receiving an Energy Star rating but didn't quite make it.

If you look at the energy and water costs for Energy Star clothes washers versus those that aren't, the difference is extraordinary. I saw a Maytag washer with the Energy Star label that was selling for $999.99. Its companion dryer was $599.99. The pair was projected to use $24 a year in electricity when used with an electric water heater or $11 a year when used with a gas water heater. That's great. But it would be pretty easy to buy a good washer-dryer combo for $600, or $1,000 less than the Energy Star pair. That's a lot more to pay for an energy savings of maybe $50 a year.

If you pay more for an appliance to save on energy usage, try to get an appliance that saves you enough on energy in three years to equal the extra cost. So if the Energy Star appliance costs $120 more, make sure you save at least $40 a year on energy or water use. Check www.energystar.gov, and click "calculate my savings" to see when you should buy an energy-efficient appliance. As manufacturers get better at manufacturing these appliances, it will make more and more sense to buy one. It's also not bad for the environment.

Sometimes there are rebates available for buying Energy Star appliances. Check energystar.gov for rebate information.

The second most important characteristic of an appliance is its reliability. Certain brands are much more reliable than others, and with something as expensive and potentially long-lived as a refrigerator, you want one that will perform reliably and not require costly repairs. Normally I don't care about brand names, but in this case, brand names really do matter.

The best place to find out which brands are reliable and which are not is

Consumer Reports (www.consumerreports. org). *Consumer Reports* surveys its readers to find out what problems they've had with appliances, and reports those brand repair histories. It's interesting that, even across different appliances, some brands tend to be relatively trouble-free, while other brands are likely to have problems. For example, Frigidaire and Amana show up in the CR ratings as being more likely to break down, whether the appliance is a refrigerator/freezer, dishwasher, washing machine, or clothes dryer. On the other hand, Whirlpool and Kenmore are consistently among the most reliable appliances.

It's hard to buy a specific model based on *Consumer Reports* reviews, because the model numbers change by the time the magazine hits the newsstands. It's really more a problem with electronics than appliances. But the magazine's general information is really good—how you decide on features, ease of use, and quality brands.

Sometimes two brands can be one and the same, at different prices. Different brands are manufactured by the same company and marketed to different buyers at different prices. For example, the refrigerator I just bought was a Hotpoint, but it was identical to the GE refrigerator displayed about fifteen feet away. I asked the salesperson what the difference was between the two and, after checking the catalog, he acknowledged that they were identical. But the GE cost $80 more—a total of $879—than the $799 Hotpoint. Was I going to pay $80 more for the GE? No way.

One warning here for people who might be buyers of high-end homes. In that market, there's been an obsession with ultra-premium appliances, and buying these appliances is a very bad idea. We had the misfortune of inheriting a house full of a particular brand of ultra-high-end appliances, and every one of them broke before the normal life cycle of similar appliances. We had to replace everything: the oven, refrigerator, cooktop, and dishwasher. I figured it was just bad luck, but in *Consumer Reports*, the ultra-high-end appliances are by far the lowest-rated in terms of reliability. That may be because these appliances are produced in smaller quantities, before manufacturers have figured out the best way to make them. That's the reason you shouldn't buy a car in the first model-year, before the manufacturer works out the bugs.

Ironically, we bought a beach house whose kitchen was full of the same appliances we had to replace back home, and sure enough, those appliances are failing and we're replacing every one.

If you're building a high-end house or remodeling your kitchen, don't buy one of the built-in oven/microwave combinations, because there's a danger of permanently installing obsolete technology. Put in a unit with two ovens instead, and use a counter-top microwave.

Most appliances are extremely reliable, and that will be especially true if you've selected brands that are known for reliability. So it is a terrible waste of money to buy a service contract on them. It would be far better to keep the money you would spend on all those service contracts in your pocket and use it to make the rare repair. That's true for appliances and electronics.

The best places to buy appliances are low-cost outlets such as Home Depot and Lowe's, which have decided they want to own the appliance market. They have Sears quaking in its boots, and Sears's market share is shrinking. But Home Depot and Lowe's are afraid of Wal-Mart, the nation's largest retailer, which is selling major appliances in more and more of its stores. Home Depot and Lowe's have very good prices, although they're not the cheapest prices. They do offer end-to-end service, just as you would get at Sears. They deliver the appliance, set it up, and haul away the old one. You can buy appliances at Sam's Club or Costco and get a lower price (BJ's sells appliances in only some of its stores), but then you're going to have to figure out how to get it home, how to install it, and how to haul away the old appliance, and that has held back their appliance sales. Lowe's and Home Depot sometimes offer free delivery as they compete with each other, but delivery isn't the same as delivery, setup, and haul-away. If you're like me and are incapable of hooking up anything, make sure the price you pay includes all three. If you want a great price and are able to do things yourself, try Sam's and Costco first. Sam's and Costco do offer delivery by a third-party service, for a fee, and they often double the warranty you would get elsewhere. But Home Depot and Lowe's offer the best combination of price and convenience. Wal-Mart is still a wild card.

• Tips on Appliances •

○ Consider an appliance's energy usage and its repair record as two of the top criteria in making a purchase, along with price and features.

○ If you pay more for an Energy Star appliance, make sure the energy savings each year will allow you to make back the extra cost in three years or less.

○ Check *Consumer Reports* brand repair histories to find brands that are likely to be reliable.

○ Avoid ultra-premium appliances, because they tend to break down most frequently.

○ Home Depot and Lowe's offer good prices for appliances and end-to-end service. They deliver the appliance, set it up, and haul away the old appliance.

• Internet •

www.consumerreports.org

www.energystar.gov

CHAPTER 6

EVENTS

Some events happen once in a lifetime, others once a year. No matter what the frequency, a little advance planning can make a big difference in how much you enjoy the event, and how enjoyable it is for your wallet.

There are so many ways that weddings, parties, and other events can be done more affordably. The events you have time to plan are the ones that provide the best opportunity to save money. They're also the ones that can get us in the most trouble, because of the endless options. You lose track of your original goals and get caught up in lots of tempting possibilities. You reach just a little farther and deeper into your wallet.

Instead, take a step back as you plan an event, and think about what you remember most and enjoyed most about special functions you attended. Very likely it was the people you got to be with and the event itself, not every tiny detail. Keep that in perspective as you plan.

As long as you keep people well fed, all the rest is less significant. Come up with your budget and stick to it.

The same applies to shopping for annual events like birthdays and Christmas. You'll read a lot in this section about how to plan, how to budget, and how to save. I hope you'll take some of it to heart.

* PARTIES *

If you're planning a big party—a graduation or engagement party or perhaps a religious celebration—you'll find a wide range of prices on catering facilities. And the way to find the best deal is old-fashioned digging. You have to call place after place after place, and along the way you'll discover more questions to ask.

One way to save is to take advantage of the weekly calendar. If you're planning a weekend event, you can steal a deal on space at an airport hotel, or a hotel that caters to conventions, because they're not as busy on the weekends as they are during the week. They want you to book a Friday night or Saturday night event, and they'll negotiate to get your event.

We're having a big party for my thirteen-year-old daughter, Rebecca, at a luxury hotel, because it was the cheapest place I could find—about a third cheaper than the next cheapest place. The hotel caters to business travelers and has no weekend business at all. The space was going to be empty anyway, so they basically waive the facilities charge. Then you pay the same food mark-up as you would anyplace else. If you live in a city that has a lot of conventions, contact the local convention and visitors bureau and get a schedule of major conventions. Schedule your special event when there are no big conventions in town.

On the other hand, you can save tons of money on events that traditionally are celebrated on the weekend, such as weddings, by shifting them to other nights of the week. Don't laugh. A lot of brides actually are moving their weddings from Friday or Saturday night to Tuesday night or Thursday night, because of the incredible amount of money they can save by doing that. (For more on how to save on weddings, see the Weddings section of this book.)

Ask the restaurant or catering manager: "I know that's your price for Saturday, but what would your price be if we did it on Sunday? What would be the price if we did it on Thursday?" Thursday's becoming a big event night because it's near the end of the work week, like Friday, but it's a lot cheaper. It doesn't sound as strange to people as having an event on Monday.

If you're planning to have music at your event, you might be surprised to find out how inexpensive it is now to have a disc jockey versus a live band. The cost of the equipment has declined so much that a lot more people are working as party DJs, and that competition has driven the price down. I hired a DJ for Rebecca's party, an on-air personality from a local radio station, for just $450 with karaoke.

If you're hiring a live band, or maybe just a keyboardist, it's critical to hear them play, and not hire just on price. If you don't like how they sound, the price doesn't matter.

The same is true for food. It's easy to compare one menu to another, but if you don't like the food, price is irrelevant. A caterer should give you free samples. If the event will be at a restaurant, go eat there before you decide. Generally, you'll spend less money having the celebration at a restaurant than having a caterer come to your facility or your home. Surprisingly, having hot hors d'oeuvres isn't necessarily a bargain. If you're looking to stretch the budget and still serve people a substantial amount of food, a buffet is more cost effective than having hors d'oeuvres carried around by servers.

You can save money on every phase of a big party. Take flowers, for example. For Rebecca's party, we're going to buy the flowers ourselves on the day of the event and take them to the hotel instead of hiring a florist. That's going to cut the cost of flowers by about 80 percent.

Because laser printers are so good, it's now possible for you to print your own party invitations. You can design the invitation using something as simple as Microsoft Word. Print a draft on cheap paper first until you get a final version, and then laser-print the invitations onto blank invitation paper you can buy at a party store. By doing it this way, you can drive the cost down to fifteen to twenty cents per invitation, or less than twenty dollars for one hundred invitations.

You can also buy party invitations online. Go to your favorite search engine and search for "party invitations." Pick any site, pick out an invitation style you like, and fill it out online. You can see exactly what it would look like, and then buy it. The finished invitations will show up in a few weeks, sooner if you put in a rush order. So there's no more going to the typesetter and reviewing proofs. By cutting out the labor and going to this semi-automated process, you can reduce the cost tremendously.

There's another option for a surprise birthday party or a housewarming—

definitely not for a wedding—and that is "e-vites" (or one of their competitors), the online invitations that you e-mail to your guests. I think they're really cute, and in this age, when people often don't bother to RSVP to a party, e-vites allow you to send follow-up reminders, and allow guests to RSVP by e-mail. That brings the RSVP rate to close to 100 percent. They're fun, free, and convenient.

You can save money on decorations by doing them yourself, and that doesn't mean you have to paint murals on your walls. The place might not look like a million bucks, but it might look like a hundred thousand bucks, and you've spent only a few dollars. For a child's birthday, the local dollar store is a great place to find party decorations, party favors, and wrapping paper. Party stores are pretty expensive, but still a lot cheaper than hiring someone to do it.

For a smaller party, maybe a housewarming or a going-away party for a co-worker, you can handle the food affordably and conveniently with food trays, available at supermarkets and the warehouse clubs. My brothers and I took full advantage of party trays when we agreed to arrange a hospitality suite for my nephew's wedding. You buy them in advance and pick them up. They're about twenty bucks a tray and each tray feeds a lot of people and looks terrific. You can get fruit trays, meat trays, cheese trays, and vegetable trays. You probably could make a cheese tray yourself and save a few dollars—but these things really are great and a good value.

• Tips on Parties •

❍ Shop around for the best deals on catering halls. Use the calendar to your advantage. Book a convention hotel on the weekend, or ask other catering halls if they will charge less if you hold the event on a weeknight.

❍ A disc jockey is a much cheaper alternative to live music. If you do decide on a band, listen to it play first.

❍ For huge savings, buy flowers yourself instead of hiring a florist.

❍ Print invitations yourself on a laser printer, or use invitations you can create online.

❍ The local dollar store is a great place to buy decorations for a child's birthday party.

❍ Party trays, available at supermarkets and warehouse clubs, are a good food choice for a smaller party.

• Internet •

www.evite.com

A wedding is a once-in-a-lifetime event, and it carries a once-in-a-lifetime price tag. The average wedding in the United States costs about $20,000—so much money that a lot of couples are choosing instead to elope.

One of the hottest trends in the wedding industry is to combine the wedding and honeymoon. My nephew and his bride did this. They got married—and had their honeymoon—in Belize. This started in Las Vegas, the wedding capital of the United States, and now resort communities in the Caribbean, Hawaii, and elsewhere are doing a huge business in combo wedding/honeymoons. You can have family come along and attend the ceremony, then go home. Or you can have a private ceremony, then hold a party back home after the honeymoon is over. If you're having a private ceremony, the resort may include the wedding for a few hundred dollars more than the cost of your stay, or less. It could be as little as

$50. So you can save nearly all the cost of the wedding, thousands of dollars.

If you want a more traditional wedding, the first thing to decide is how much you can afford to spend. If your parents are paying, ask them what they're willing to spend. And check on what the groom's family might be willing to contribute. If you're paying for your own wedding, check your savings or figure out how much you could save by the wedding date, and figure out a bottom-line amount.

Some couples start the opposite way, by looking at reception sites, wedding dresses, and musicians, and have no idea how much it will all add up to. If you don't budget an amount first, you'll get totally mixed up.

Wedding Web sites such as www.theknot.com will show you all of the potential expenses of a wedding. Once you have a bottom-line number, you can figure out how much of the total to spend on each major component. To do that, you'll have to decide your priorities. You might want to spend the money for a live band, while your fiancé might want to invite 200 of his closest friends. Since most catering facilities will charge you by the person, deciding how many people to invite will have a greater impact on the cost of the wedding than anything else. If you and your partner have widely different goals, someone is going to have to compromise.

Theknot.com has a budgeting tool that will help you turn your bottom-line figure into a detailed budget. You tell it how much you want to spend on the wedding and how much you plan to spend on a few components, and it will tell you how much you have left to spend on other parts of the wedding. Then you can make adjustments.

The reception is the most expensive component, and your budget will help you decide what kind of reception to have. A sit-down dinner, for example, would be a lot more expensive than a brunch or a dessert/champagne reception. You could spend $300 a person for a very fancy sit-down dinner, which for 100 people would be $30,000—just for the meal.

You'll also have to consider the cost of entertainment, the wedding dress, flowers, invitations, limousines, alcohol, and photography.

There are lots of ways to save on the cost of a wedding. As I note in the section on parties, you can save tons of money on a wedding by having it on a Tuesday or Thursday night instead of a Saturday. If that's too extreme, get married on a Friday or Sunday. A lot of people are doing that. Just keep in mind that if you're going to have a lot of out-of-town guests, they might not be able to make it in for a mid-week wedding. Or you could save by having your wedding in January instead of June, which is one of the most popular months for weddings. If you avoid the most popular months, you may have more negotiating power.

Christa DiBiase, the executive producer of my radio show and our in-house expert on weddings, knows all the tricks. At her wedding, for example, she spent a lot less on alcohol than most people, yet still had a full bar. She did that by buying the alcohol herself at a discount store and bringing it to the reception. Photography was very important to Christa, so she spent more on that, but she didn't spend a lot on her dress. She brought in her own caterer, and saved money there.

The bride wants everything to be perfect on her wedding day, but that doesn't mean she can't have that beautiful wedding on a budget. If you look at all the great ideas in wedding magazines and books, you can duplicate almost anything on a budget. Perhaps you have a friend who is a talented artist. As her wedding gift to you, she could make the flower arrangements, so you won't have to spend a fortune paying a florist.

Here are some other ways to save:

Bridal Magazines

Because most women buy up to twenty bridal magazines to scour for ideas and tips, the cost can really add up. You can get all that information for free by visiting your local library. You won't want a pile of magazines or expensive coffee-table bridal books after you're married, so why pay for them? Christa saw a book at her library by the famed wedding designer Colin Cowie, and others by Martha Stewart and Vera Wang. Also, ask friends who were married recently if they still have their books and magazines. After Christa got married, she tied a bow around all of her bridal magazines and gave them to a friend who was getting married.

Dresses

If you really want the fairy-tale dress but don't want to spend a fortune, consider renting a dress, borrowing one, or buying a used dress at a consignment store. If you go to "sample sales" and buy a dress off the rack, you can get a designer dress for half its regular price. One of Christa's friends cut out pictures of designer dresses she liked, bought the fabric at a fabric outlet, and hired a seamstress to make a copy. It cost her a total of $300 to get a fabulous custom-made dress. A department store is another place to look. They have a lot of great off-the-rack dresses. For some reason with wedding dresses, the simpler and more elegant the dress is, the more it costs. Dresses with a lot of lace and beading don't cost as much. If you buy at a fancy wedding shop, don't customize the dress too much (for example, ask for a different style of sleeves) or you'll pay a lot more.

A few times a year, I get a phone call from a distressed bride-to-be, or often from her mother, about a problem with a wedding dress. Rachel was one such caller. Her daughter's wedding was in one week, and the dress wasn't in the store yet. They had been promised that it would arrive a month before the wedding. The bridal store kept giving her empty promises, and she wanted some help.

This is precisely why I hate custom-ordered wedding dresses. I've had calls about stores that went out of business overnight, leaving brides stranded without dresses, veils, and bridesmaids' dresses. Sometimes there is nothing

that can be done. In Rachel's case, there was a solution.

She had purchased the dress using a credit card fifty-eight days before she called me. She had two more days to put the dress into dispute on her credit card. If the store couldn't deliver the dress on time, then at least she would be able to get her money back. But her daughter had her heart set on that particular dress, and since the sample dress had fit her in the store, she bought that dress, and the store gave her a discount. The store also agreed to have the dress professionally cleaned, rush the alterations, and do them at no additional charge.

Flowers

A friend of Christa's had her mother do the flowers, using a Martha Stewart book as a guide. The end result was spectacular. Even if you use a florist, you can save. Before Christa chose her florist, she asked first if she could buy the bowls in which to display them. The florist would have charged $24 a bowl. Christa bought them for $1 each at the discount store Garden Ridge.

Invitations

As I say in the section on parties, you can print your own invitations with a laser printer, and they look just as good as engraved invitations and cost a lot less. Print them onto blank invitation paper you can buy at a party store.

Limousines

If you haven't priced a limousine in a while, you'll be shocked at the cost: about $80 an hour for a six-passenger stretch limo. If you want the limo mainly for the photos, rent one for an hour, or if there's a minimum, for the shortest time that's allowed. You can have the limo take you from the wedding to the reception and have pictures taken of you getting into and out of it. But you don't need it to pick you up after the reception, or shuttle you around before the wedding. You can ask a friend with a nice car to do that. Limousine companies frequently go out of business, so don't pay any money in advance unless you use a credit card, and make the deposit within 60 days of the date you'll need the limo (so you can do a chargeback if the company disappears).

Another alternative is to rent a really nice car and drive yourself. You can rent a luxury car for a day at any of the car rental companies and it will cost you less than renting a limo for one hour. When I checked for a weekend in Chicago, you could rent a luxury car for $54.99 from Avis, and $59.99 from Budget and National. A Lincoln Town Car is one of the most popular choices for this.

The Reception

You can save the cost of a catering hall by holding the reception at your home or someone else's home. Sometimes people who met at college will hold the reception on campus. Or check to see if you can rent a museum or other public facility for your wedding.

If you're on a very tight budget, you

could have a very small, elegant reception, and after your honeymoon invite everyone over for a big backyard barbecue. So you have the huge party but spend a lot less money than if you had a huge sit-down dinner. Some people have the reception at the church. There's no facility charge for that.

You can save a lot if you hold the reception at a place that will let you bring in your own caterer and alcohol. Some catering halls charge a minimal fee for the space, then gouge you on the food and drink. The catering hall Christa rented for her wedding charged $1,500 for the space and let her bring in her own caterer and alcohol. A fancy hall might charge $4,000 for the space, and require you to use their caterer and alcohol.

You can save by choosing what time of day you have the wedding. If you have a morning wedding, you can have a brunch with champagne, or you can have a luncheon, or a mid-afternoon wedding with appetizers only. Or you can do a late-night wedding with dessert. The most expensive choice by far is the 5:30 P.M. wedding with a full-course meal

and a band. That's when you have to spend the big bucks.

Entertainment

Do you want a disc jockey or a live band? There's a huge difference in price. You can have a DJ for a few hundred dollars, while a band will cost thousands. A well-known, top-flight band could cost $5,000 to $10,000 or more. Christa wanted a band, but that was something she compromised on for her wedding. She wanted other things more. Christa had a DJ for the event, but she snuck some live music in by hiring a piano major from a nearby college to play at a cocktail reception before the wedding. He wore a tuxedo and played for two hours, and it cost Christa just $100. A college near you might have a student jazz ensemble that will perform for much less money than a professional band.

Photography

Photographs help you remember your wedding day, so good ones are important. I get calls all the time from newly-weds whose photographer didn't show up at the wedding, took bad pictures, went out of business, or simply ran off and never delivered the pictures. The only way to protect yourself from that kind of disaster is to have some kind of backup. A lot of people put disposable cameras on every table and ask their guests to take pictures and leave the cameras for the bride and groom to have developed. You can buy them in bulk for maybe $5 each. Ask your friends who like to take pictures to shoot certain things, such as the wedding vows or the best man's toast. Christa's father took the photos for her aunt's wedding, and her aunt still hasn't forgiven him, thirty years later, because all the pictures are blurry or have his thumb in them. There is not a single decent photo of the entire event. Always have backup.

Christa got the photographer to give her the proofs of photos she didn't choose, and all the negatives. That's a huge money saver, because if you have the negatives you won't have to pay for fancy laboratory reprints. You can get the fancy photographer's album, at a cost of $600 or $700, or you can get the photographer's proofs, make reprints yourself, and create your own album. But don't skimp too much on pictures. Make sure you have a photographer who knows what they're doing.

The same is true for videography. Make sure you have someone who knows what they're doing, and have a backup. If you'd like some video but don't want the cost of a videographer, ask a relative with a good video camera to shoot the wedding for you.

Most people love having a wedding video in which their friends are interviewed and there is video of the actual wedding. But some people find the presence of the videographer too intrusive.

Once you get the video, remove the erasure-protection tabs so you don't accidentally tape over your wedding video. And make a copy.

The average wedding video costs $1,000, according to *Bridal Bargains*, by Denise and Alan Fields, but can vary from as little as $300 for a one-camera, unedited video if you live in a small town. However, a sophisticated, highly edited, multi-camera "wedding movie" could cost $2,000 to $5,000, according to the Fields book.

When you choose what kind of wedding to have, think about what really matters to you. Are you going to remember what vases the flowers were in, or are you going to want really good pictures to keep? Is a video of the wedding or a live band more important? You can save money on every aspect of the wedding. Spend the money on the things you really want. Save it on everything else.

You can find more ideas in books such as *Bridal Bargains,* at theknot.com, or on online message boards.

Planning

Time is your ally in planning a wedding. Christa planned hers in about ten months—the average probably is a year. If you want to get married sooner, it might cost you more.

Hiring a formal wedding planner is a big expense, and one you may want to avoid. If you don't want to spend the money on one, ask a friend who's not a bridesmaid to hold on to all the contracts (and bring them to the wedding) and to keep charge of the wedding checklist. If the caterer says they weren't supposed to bring pork tenderloin and they were, you don't want to worry about it. You want your friend to pull out the contract and show the caterer the pork tenderloin clause. Make sure to thank your friend in the same manner as you would a bridesmaid.

Good planning and organization helped one of my callers a lot. Jenny had planned the perfect wedding and reception for more than a year. Everything went smoothly until they reached the reception hall. She had been very specific both on the phone and in writing to the caterer that no pine nuts were to be used in any of the food. Jenny has a severe life-threatening allergy to them. Minutes into the reception, Jenny bit into her meal and tasted pine nuts. She had to leave her own reception to go to the hospital.

After writing a letter to the reception hall (the caterer was part of the hall's package), and showing them her instructions to the caterer as well as her hospital bill, all of her money was refunded for the reception. The reason Jenny was able to get a refund so swiftly is that she documented everything. Her instructions to the caterer were clear and in writing.

Her memory of that evening cannot be refunded, but I am happy to report that she used the refunded reception money toward a down payment on a new home, turning a difficult situation into an investment in her future.

• Tips on Weddings •

○ By having both the wedding and honeymoon at a resort, you can save thousands of dollars.

○ With a traditional wedding, the first thing to decide is how much you can afford to spend. If your parents are paying, ask them what they're willing to spend.

○ The reception is the most expensive component. A sit-down dinner is a lot more expensive than a brunch or a dessert/champagne reception.

○ You can save tons of money by having your wedding on a Tuesday or Thursday night instead of a Saturday. Or you can save by having your wedding in January instead of June.

○ It's possible to save money on every aspect of the wedding, including music, flowers, limo, invitations, and photography.

www.theknot.com

✳ CHRISTMAS SHOPPING ✳

The Christmas season is a dangerous time for your wallet. You're in the stores looking for the perfect gift for family and friends, and you see a few things you like for yourself as well. The result is, you end up buying more than you planned, and spending too much.

You can help resist that temptation by starting your holiday shopping with a plan. Put together a list of everyone you want to buy a gift for, including yourself. Then decide how much money you can realistically afford to spend on everyone, including yourself. Don't budget more for gifts than you can pay for right away, or certainly by the end of February. I'd prefer that you don't borrow at all for Christmas, but the reality is that a lot of people do. Still, I don't want you to become one of the people

who's still paying for last Christmas a year later.

After you have the total, whether it's $100 or $3,000, write down next to each person's name how much you expect to spend on them. If the individual totals exceed your budget, you have to either strike some people off your list or start cutting how much you're going to spend. Some people think budgeting takes some of the fun out of Christmas. But spending too much for gifts is kind of like drinking too much on New Year's Eve. You end up with a painful hangover the next day.

Keep your list on a sheet of paper that's small enough to carry with you when you go shopping. Men should keep the list in their wallet, women in their wallet or purse. That way you can refer to the list as you shop, and adjust it if need be. If you spend more on someone than you intended, you can subtract from someone else.

When to Shop

A lot of people ask me whether they should start their shopping on the frenzied first day after Thanksgiving, when some stores open at 7 A.M. and crowds wait outside to get in. If you use a list to shop and if you can handle the crowds, that first "official" shopping day and the weekend that follows really is a brilliant time to buy. Stores offer some fantastic deals in the early-morning darkness of the Friday after Thanksgiving. One year I bought a 19-inch stereo TV at Kmart for $69—by far the lowest price I've ever seen for that kind of TV. Of course, the reason they offer those deals is to get you into the store to buy other things. If you play the game right, you'll score some great deals. Just stick to your list, not necessarily the items, but the people and the money. You may get into a store and find an advertised special you over-

looked, or an unadvertised special that could be a better deal than what you had planned to buy.

Most Christmas shopping occurs the week before Christmas, not right after Thanksgiving. And that's an odd time to shop because some items will be at their most expensive, while others will be their most affordable. Anything that's seasonal—a Christmas sweater or decoration perhaps—will be on sale the week before Christmas. Electronics items tend to be extra pricey at the last minute, because that's when the panic buyers, not price-conscious buyers, are shopping. That's true of jewelry as well.

The very best time to buy is about January 10, for the following Christmas. The sale fliers make it look like the best bargains are the week between Christmas and New Year's Day. But so many people have that week off from work that they use the after-Christmas sales as an excuse to go shop some more. If you wait until Jan. 10, the stuff that really didn't sell is available at great prices, there's no traffic, and the stores are empty. Go ahead and make your list then and get what you need. My wife and I do most of the year's Christmas shopping before January has ended.

Some people like to pick up a few gifts throughout the year, maybe while they're on vacation. But that's not going to work unless you've already made out your list. Without your list, you may buy something and then forget you've bought it, or you'll overspend.

Trees

Artificial Christmas trees now vastly outsell "real" Christmas trees. If you're interested in buying an artificial Christmas tree, you can save a lot of money by waiting until January to buy it. You won't have the tree for this season, but you will have it for years and years to come.

The best bargains on real Christmas trees are at the two big home-improvement retailers: Home Depot and Lowe's. They've become enormous sellers of Christmas trees, hurting sales at the independent lots. It's a great strategy for the stores. They simply convert their garden centers into Christmas centers. They have a pretty wide selection and their prices are fantastic, with most trees selling for $19 to $29.

I recommend you buy a Christmas tree early rather than late, because you'll get a better selection and you'll be able to display the tree longer, so your cost-per-day of owning it will be less. In some parts of the country, people buy their Christmas tree on Christmas Eve, or the week before Christmas. In other regions, people buy their tree right after Thanksgiving. Whatever the regional preference, if you buy early you'll get the best deal. Just keep it watered, so you don't create a fire hazard.

Toys

A big part of Christmas for many families is buying toys for the kids. And that's where a lot of money can go down the drain—on expensive, high-tech toys your kids may not even like. I did a toy test for a TV report that was fascinating. We bought hundreds of toys, then brought together different groups of children and parents. The children played with the toys (they didn't know any of the brand names) and the parents observed and kept score of what the kids liked. To their amazement, and also to mine, the toys children played with the longest and enjoyed the most were the "classic" toys that have stood the test of time. They liked the train sets, doctor kits, and dolls—not the latest, greatest, heavily advertised toys. I was blown away, because it didn't come out at all like I expected. Because kids are so bombarded with advertising, I was sure they would prefer the toys they'd heard about on TV. The kids did play first with toys they had seen on TV, but they lost interest in those toys quickly. Then they played with the toys that required more imagination.

The neatest thing about these classic toys is that many retailers now offer copies under their private labels, good-quality stuff that's very inexpensive. I put together a Top Ten list of the kids' favorites, and many of the toys could be purchased for $9 to $15 at stores like Wal-Mart. It isn't necessary at all for parents to spend a lot of money to buy gifts that make their children happy. Kids will beg you for specific gifts, things they probably will get bored with before long. If you can afford it, you might buy one of those ad-driven items, but fill out the rest of your list with classic toys.

• Clark's Toy Test 2001: Top Ten Toys •

1. **Sock'em Boppers ($9)**
2. **Kid Connection (Wal-Mart) Animal World Playset ($15)**
3. **Kid Connection (Wal-Mart) Electronic Cash Register ($10)**
4. **(Tie) Kid Connection (Wal-Mart) Vehicle Adventure Kit Police and Fire ($15)**
5. **Kid Connection (Wal-Mart) Vehicle Adventure Kit Military ($15)**
6. **Nerf Ultra-Grip Football ($10)**

7. **Matchbox Hero Highway ($39)**

8. **Fisher-Price Great Adventure Pirate Ship ($28)**

9. **Pixter ($30)**

10. **Diva Starz ($21)**

Jewelry

A lot of people buy jewelry at Christmas, often men buying for their wives or girlfriends. Jewelry is a very subjective purchase, because it's almost impossible to know the quality or value of a $100 necklace or a $200 bracelet. Most of the jewelry that people buy as holiday gifts costs $50 to $200, and in that price range, the best thing to do is look for a style you like, or one that you think the recipient will like, and try to compare it in price with similar items at other stores. Don't worry about the "70 percent off" sales. Look at the price of the item, not what they say is the discount, because stores often will mark up to mark down. So 70 percent off a fake price doesn't mean anything. What matters is that essentially the same earrings are $69 in one store, $49 in another.

It's important to find a few stores that sell the kind of jewelry you like, and have prices you think are reasonable. For jewelry priced at less than $200, I love Tuesday Morning, a chain of stores that's open only certain times of the year. All the Tuesday Morning stores stock jewelry, but there's a much wider range of choices in some than in others. Value City is another option. It's a national discounter with a fairly limited selection of jewelry at prices that are really pleasing. Of the warehouse clubs, BJ's has the most jewelry, but Sam's Club is making a major push. And believe it or not, Wal-Mart is now the largest seller of jewelry in the country.

The warehouse clubs have really changed the equation, because their markups are so small.

If you're buying a piece of jewelry for $2,000 or more, the kind you would want to have insured, it makes sense to use an independent appraiser to verify the quality and value of the piece. It's a lot trickier when you're looking at jewelry that costs $500, $600, or $800. That's the never-never land for jewelry, because that's a lot of money but not enough to bring in an appraiser.

The Better Business Bureau has a brochure that includes pages of information and tips on how to buy jewelry. It's available by mail for a small fee, or you can print a copy from its Web site, www.bbb.org. The brochure is a little hard to find on the site. The direct link to it is www.bbb.org/library/jewelry.asp.

Among the information in the BBB brochure are the color and clarity ratings for diamonds from the Gemological Institute of America. It also includes information about jewelry repairs; precious metals such as gold, platinum, and silver; pearls, and colored gemstones such as emeralds, rubies, and sapphires.

Gift Certificates

If you don't know what to buy somebody, you might decide to give a gift certificate or a gift card. A lot of money is being spent on these—nearly $40 billion a year—and I don't like that at all.

When you buy a gift certificate, you're taking actual U.S. money and turning it into an I.O.U. from a particular store that may not stay in business. Or you might get a gift certificate from a store your friend or family member doesn't enjoy. Amazingly, many gift certificates now have expiration dates. So if they don't use the gift certificate in time, it's worthless. My co-author, Mark Meltzer, won a $50 gift certificate as a prize for being in a bowling tournament at work. The gift certificate was for a mall about thirty minutes from Mark's house. He doesn't shop at malls much, and didn't realize the gift certificate had an expiration date. When he finally thought about using it, he saw that it had expired.

Some stores also charge fees to buy a gift card, or they charge monthly or per-use fees for using them. So you can turn $100 into $91. It's a complete rip-off.

I prefer that you give cash, because there's nothing more personal about a gift certificate than cash. You won't find an expiration date on a $20 bill, or incur a fee for using one. Don't trade money for something that's inferior.

Occasionally, you'll get a gift from the store if you buy a gift certificate. If it's something you want, and you can get more out of your dollar by buying the gift certificate, that may be a worthwhile trade. Otherwise, no way.

$100 or Less

One way to deal with the heavy emphasis on spending money during Christmas is to adopt a different philosophy. Michele Singletary, a syndicated personal financial writer, writes eloquently about the true meaning of Christmas, and she advocates spending no more than $100 for your entire Christmas budget. Her approach is to make things for people, bake things for people, and spend time with people. I love that idea, not necessarily because I'm thrifty, but because we really have lost the meaning of the holiday in all the merchandising. She believes the

holiday should be a celebration with family and friends, not about who can put the most on their Visa card.

Singletary writes about ten columns a year, starting around Halloween, about people's reactions to her approach. She has friends and relatives who get upset with her. But why not try it? Think how much stuff you get that you don't like and never use. And it's harder than ever for people to return gifts to the store. So a lot of money spent on Christmas presents is just wasted.

Returns

Whenever you buy a gift for someone, there's always the possibility it won't fit or they won't like it, and they'll want to return it. Unfortunately, returns, refunds, and exchanges have become the Achilles' heel of gift shopping and personal shopping.

Retailers have become more reluctant to take returns, in part because of the growing danger that they will take back merchandise that was stolen. Because of bar codes and high employee turnover, it's become a lot easier for rings of criminals to steal from the stores. They don't need a gun, and they can walk off with tens of thousands of dollars in merchandise or cash in just a few days.

The crooks will get one or more of their members hired as a cashier. Then they'll print up their own bar codes, place their sticker over the original sticker, and a member of the ring will take an expensive item up to a register manned by one of his colleagues. So a $300 item rings up as $3, and the crook walks right out the door. Later, he takes off the temporary sticker, takes the item back for a refund, and says he has no receipt.

Retailers have responded to this type of theft by limiting the number of returns everyone is allowed in a year, or every few months. That's a big problem if you've received a number of gifts for Christmas or a wedding that you need to return. Stores won't let you exchange or refund the item, not even for store credit, unless you have the original receipt, or what's known as a "gift receipt." A lot of retailers now give you an actual receipt and a second receipt, which lists the item but no price. When you give a gift, you're supposed to include the gift receipt so that the recipient can return it if they need to. This cumbersome system has spread throughout retailing, because every time one retailer becomes more refund-friendly than another, the criminal rings migrate to that retailer.

If you look, you'll see that retailers with centralized checkouts now have their cameras monitoring each cashier, not shoplifting that may occur in the interior of the store. And if you're wondering why some stores now have people checking your receipt when you leave, it's to try to catch these bar-code crime rings.

The warehouse clubs do this, but they're a lot harder for the theft rings to hit because you have to be a member to shop there. So they can track purchases and returns based on your member number. I think stores should give people the option of being able to register as a member and pay a small charge for it.

As a consumer, you have to make sure you find out the return policy of each store you shop at, especially if you're shopping for a gift. Keep your own receipts, and check for time limits on returns. Some stores may require you to return an item within fourteen days or sixty days, and some will give you less than you paid if the item has been discounted since you bought it. If a gift receipt is needed, make sure you include it with the gift.

Returning electronics items is more difficult also, whether the item is a gift or something you bought for yourself. It's become a nightmare actually, as retailers are now charging "restocking fees." Even if you return an item unopened, you could be charged a restocking fee of 15 to 25 percent of the purchase price. Retailers who sell computers and electronics say prices drop so quickly that people often return things just to take advantage of a new, lower price. Costco has a policy I like a lot, although they don't publicize it. If an item you buy there drops in price within 30 days of when you bought it, you can bring your receipt back and they'll refund the difference. Some other stores will do that as well. So if you buy an item on Saturday and the Sunday sales circular has the same thing at 20 percent less, they'll give you the difference rather than making you return it and buy it again.

• Tips on Christmas Shopping •

- ○ Make a list of the people you want to buy for, figure a budget for all, then write down how much of the total you'll spend on each person. Include something for yourself.

- ○ Carry the list with you when you shop, and make adjustments to it along the way.

- The day after Thanksgiving is a great time to land some deals, if you can handle the crowds.

- Be careful the week before Christmas. Seasonal items are cheap, but electronics and jewelry are expensive.

- Buy classic, inexpensive toys for children, instead of the expensive, heavily advertised stuff. Kids prefer these toys, and they're much easier on your budget.

- For the typical holiday jewelry purchase, $50 to $200, find something you like and don't worry about quality. Compare prices among stores, but ignore "70 percent off" sales. Retailers mark up, then mark down, so the percentages mean nothing.

- Shop for jewelry at discounters such as Tuesday Morning, Value City, Wal-Mart, or the warehouse clubs: Sam's Club, BJ's, and Costco.

- Find out stores' return policies, and don't give gifts that can't be returned. Include a gift receipt with your gift if the store requires that for a return.

✳ VALENTINE'S DAY ✳

Valentine's Day can be an expensive occasion for a guy who wants to show how much he loves his sweetheart. Having a bouquet of roses delivered by a florist can cost $100 or more.

But there's another way that's more personal and much cheaper: Bring the flowers yourself to your wife or girlfriend's office. I've never understood why anyone considers flowers delivered by a stranger to be a more romantic gesture than flowers delivered by your beloved.

I've found the best deals on flowers

at supermarkets, the warehouse clubs, and nurseries, for whom February is a terrible time of year. The warehouse clubs, oddly, are not as good a deal on Valentine's Day as the supermarkets and the nurseries. By buying at a non-traditional outlet, you should be able to buy a beautiful bouquet of long-stemmed roses for $19 to $29 a dozen, and save $70 or more from what a florist would charge.

Chocolates also cost more before Valentine's Day, but you can save a lot of money by waiting until Valentine's Day itself, even a couple of days before Valentine's Day, to buy. Stores get worried that they're going to get stuck with the merchandise, so they put their chocolates on clearance. It's one case where waiting until the last minute actually will save you money.

I give flowers to my wife, Lane, all the time, so she doesn't want them on Valentine's Day because she knows what a rip-off they are. Women say the most important thing is for their husband or sweetheart to do something thoughtful for them for Valentine's Day, and it doesn't have to be the standard stuff. In fact, the more creative the idea, the more it's appreciated. Try making dinner, cleaning the house, or doing something else she doesn't like to do. If you really want to get her upset, don't do anything for her on Valentine's Day.

Here's another idea. Give your sweetheart roses the week before Valentine's Day and the week after. They're so much cheaper before and after the holiday that you can give her roses twice for less. Then on Feb. 14, maybe you give her chocolates.

For Valentine's Day decorations, and decorations for any holiday except Christmas (when you have to wait until Jan. 10), you can get some incredible bargains the day after the holiday, because seasonal items are worth nothing to the retailer at that point. They just want to get rid of them. So if you're a good advance planner, you can buy your decorations for next year at 75 percent off. That's $40 worth of products for $10, quite a deal. This applies to Christmas decorations and wrapping paper, and decorations for Halloween, Easter, and St. Patrick's Day, among others.

✳ FUNERALS ✳

I wrote about funerals in my previous book, *Get Clark Smart,* and I'm going to do it again here because death is an event we all experience and, while emotionally wrenching, also involves a lot of expense. The average funeral now costs $8,000 to $10,000, including cemetery expenses.

One of the most interesting shifts is the dramatic increase in the acceptability of cremation, which generally is a much less expensive alternative to burial. One of the ironies of the infamous Tri-State Crematorium scandal in Noble, Georgia, near Chattanooga, is that in the middle of America's Bible Belt, the scandal wasn't over cremation itself, but about bodies that should have been cremated but weren't.

You may join the legions of people who are deciding to be cremated instead of buried.

If you're comfortable with cremation from a religious or personal standpoint, it is a marvelous choice. It's inexpensive and, strange as this may sound, convenient, because in an era in which people move more frequently from city to city, cremation allows you to take the remains of a loved one with you, or scatter them in a place they loved. My wife, Lane, is going to scatter my ashes at the local Costco.

So many people move away from where a loved one is buried, and never get to visit with them. Mark Meltzer recently flew to New York for a rare visit to the grave of his mother, stayed a half hour, and later flew home. Who knows when he'll get there again? Mark's mom died in 1971, and he hasn't lived in New York since 1977.

The cost of cremation varies greatly, but the cheapest, invariably, will be through the local memorial society, where you can reduce funeral costs to $500 to $1,500. That's a lot cheaper than a burial. You pay a one-time fee to join and can list your wishes and get negotiated prices for cremation, cremation urns, caskets, burials, or other services. You set the budget and pick what you want, and you spare your family the agony of having to make those choices later, when they are very vulnerable.

When you die, your family goes to the funeral home you designated and they pull the file specifying your arrangements and preset costs. The decisions you make in advance can save a fortune later. The funeral homes are willing to give great prices to the memorial society in exchange for the high volume of business generated by their relationship.

Don't put this information in your will. Tell the family members who will make these decisions what you want, and put it in writing as well.

Advance planning doesn't mean buying a funeral plot or prepaying for a funeral, both of which are very bad ideas. You might move to a different city, or the funeral home could go out of business, taking your money with it. Even worse, there have been scandals across the country in which people have prepurchased a plot, and the owner failed to maintain the cemetery. What looked like a beautiful place at the time they arranged to buy a plot later looked like an overgrown weed patch.

There's such a revolt against funeral home operators in Canada that it's created a movement called home burial. Your family actually digs your grave and buries you, completely cutting out the cemeteries and funeral homes. Home burial has spread across the border to New England. It's just wild.

Home burial is legal in the United States in all but five states, according to Lisa Carlson, author of the book *Caring for the Dead*. In addition, a family or church group may handle a death without a funeral director in all but a few states, including Connecticut, New York, Indiana, Louisiana, and Nebraska. And burying cremated remains is legal anywhere, with the land owner's permission. Home burial is very much in the American tradition, when people buried their dead on a small portion of their land. But it's best in a rural area. They're not going to let you plant Aunt Minnie twenty-five feet from a neighbor's badminton court.

Another option, which costs absolutely nothing, is to donate the body to a medical school for study. After they are done, they'll return the cremated remains to the family.

People are so uncomfortable talking about death that they don't plan ahead. Even my co-author hasn't made arrangements, for himself, his wife, or his 77-year-old father, who after all, isn't going to live forever. Mark's wife, Nancy, definitely doesn't want to be buried, but she isn't thrilled about cremation either, so Mark jokes that he's going to have her stuffed and put her in the corner of the bedroom. That's funny, but eventually they're going to have to make a decision.

It's so much better to decide this stuff ahead of time.

• Tips on Funerals •

❍ The average funeral costs $8,000 to $10,000, including cemetery costs, but a funeral prearranged through a memorial society can cost much less.

❍ Cremation is an affordable option that's growing dramatically in popularity.

❍ Plan your funeral in advance through a memorial society, but never prepay funeral expenses. You could move to another city, or the funeral home could go out of business.

• Contact •

Funeral Consumers Alliance

(For a directory of memorial societies in your area)

800-765-0107

www.funerals.org

CHAPTER 7

HOME IMPROVEMENT

I often hear from my radio listeners that they want to do something to their house—maybe add a deck or install hardwood floors—to improve its value. But in reality, there's not a single improvement you can do to a house that will increase its value by the amount you spent on the upgrade. Kitchen and bathroom improvements are the best, and they return 50 to 75 percent of the cost of the improvement, according to appraisals done by *Consumer Reports.* For example, if you spend $10,000 to remodel a bathroom, it might increase the value of your house by $5,000 to $7,500. Painting the exterior of your home or putting on a new roof has only a 10 percent return. A new deck has about a 50 percent return. So a new $5,900 deck adds just $2,950 to your home's value. From a strictly financial point of view, you're better off keeping the money. So base your decision to improve your house on what you would enjoy, not its investment value.

Most people don't think much about the money they spend to decorate, improve, and repair their house. The cost is an afterthought. But with some planning, you can save money and make your house more enjoyable to live in. And some things you thought you couldn't afford to do may seem possible with my strategies.

I don't want you to feel "house poor," where your house becomes a sinkhole that draws in every penny you have, keeping you from doing anything else. But I do want you to enjoy living in it.

Some of my ideas might seem kooky to you, like buying used furniture or using high-efficiency light bulbs. I was a guest on a radio show in Las Vegas, and the host and co-host laughed hysterically when I talked about buying used furniture. They both thought I was kidding. But read on, and maybe you'll see it my way.

✳ PAINTING ✳

If you're getting a house ready to sell, or just want to freshen it up for your own pleasure, painting a room is one of the most affordable things you can do. If you do it yourself, it could cost as little as $50 to $75 to completely change the look of a room. Of course, it might also take a lot of your time and give you a headache.

Lane and I have painted rooms ourselves and hired people to paint them, and one thing we've learned is that you can't tell from a paint sample how a color is going to look on your walls.

So here's a suggestion that will save you a lot of heartache and, potentially, a tremendous amount of money. Whether you hire a painter or do it yourself, don't go out and buy three or four gallons of paint premixed to the color of your choice. Instead, buy one gallon and paint a section of your wall with it. Make it nice and large, at least six feet by six feet, and let it dry. If you love the color, just get some more paint and you're all set. If you hate the color, you're free to try again, and all you've lost is $15 or $20. That's so much better than looking at a room that a painter has just completed and being horrified by the color you thought you wanted.

If you're going to paint a room yourself, pay attention to the prep work. Fill the little holes in your walls, then let the filler material dry, and sand it smooth. Caulk the gaps around windows and baseboards. Good preparation allows paint to last longer and look better. A good-quality paint helps the job look great. Professional painter Mark Kenady likes Sherwin-Williams, Benjamin Moore, Porter, Glidden, and Devoe paints. Expect to pay $15 to $25 a gallon.

Kenady prefers oil-based paints for trim work and in areas like the kitchen, where cleanup is important. But most do-it-yourselfers prefer water-based latex paints, because mistakes and drips are easily cleaned with soap and water. Oil paints give off fumes, and you need mineral spirits to clean yourself and your brushes. Be careful if you're not sure what kind of paint you're painting over. You can't put latex over oil without using a primer first. If you're not sure, Kenady says you should apply a little denatured alcohol to the paint. If it becomes gummy, it's oil-based paint.

As far as tools go, Kenady suggests using a paintbrush with nylon bristles for latex paint, and a roller with a ⅜-inch or ½-inch nap. A thicker nap, say ¾-inch, holds more paint, but is more likely to leave lines.

Doing the painting yourself will cost about a third the cost of using a professional, but you can't beat the convenience of bringing in a pro, who very likely will have the job finished in two or three days. You can look for a professional painter by asking neighbors or checking at the local paint store. Sometimes local homeowners associations print booklets of contractors that have been recommended by one or more of their members. When you find one who is reliable, shows up on time, and is conscientious about their work, send him or her a card at Christmas and on their birthday. Finding a good painter is almost impossible, so you want yours to really like you. When you want them to come back, they'll come back.

Many house painters do this work as a transition from one job to another, and aren't in it as a career. So you might find somebody whose work you're thrilled with, but the next time you call, they're not in the painting business anymore.

Few people paint the exterior of their home themselves anymore. That's a good time to turn to a professional. It's also a good time to consider alternatives to paint, such as vinyl or aluminum siding, which are much more long-lasting than paint.

I have a few rules to consider if you think you might like vinyl, aluminum, or some other alternative substance. First, if every house in your neighborhood has wood siding, and no one uses vinyl or aluminum, paint the house. When it's time to resell your house, buyers will see your house as inferior if all the other houses have a real wood exterior and your house has aluminum or vinyl or something else. But that won't happen if vinyl or aluminum are common in your neighborhood.

Second, if you don't plan to be in the house long enough to paint the outside three times, you're better off painting than using a "maintenance-free surface." Permanent siding costs at least double what it would cost to have a house painted, so you want to make sure you're going to be in the house a while before you spend the extra money. With the average family owning a house for five to seven years, the expense of permanent siding isn't a good choice for most people. The durability of paint varies depending on weather. You might have to repaint in as little as three years, or a paint job might last as long as seven or eight years. Three to five years is a good bet. (Make sure the painter pressure-washes the house first and have him apply two top coats of paint.)

My third rule is, use a neutral color if you choose siding, because at some point you'll want to sell your home, and you don't want a "permanent" color that some buyers might not like. I bought a house at an estate sale that hadn't sold for a long time, and one of the reasons it didn't sell was that the back of the house had vinyl siding, and the vinyl was an unattractive, pale, pasty green. The late homeowner had loved the color, but potential buyers didn't. It didn't bother me at all, but when I sold it, the buyers went so far as to replace all the siding with a new color, and paint the front of the house. That was a lot of work and expense, to replace something that was supposed to be near-permanent. If you put up siding, pick a color that's typical for the neighborhood.

• Tips on Painting •

○ Whether you hire a pro or do the paint job yourself, start by buying one gallon and paint a large section of your wall with it, to make sure you like the color. If you don't, all you're out is $10 or $20.

○ If you're painting the exterior, have the painter pressure-wash the house and apply two topcoats of paint.

○ Consider vinyl or aluminum siding if you plan to own the house for long enough that you would need to have the house painted three times.

○ If you get vinyl or aluminum siding, choose a neutral color that is common in your neighborhood.

✳ CARPET AND FLOORING ✳

When I tell people what I pay for carpet, they do a double-take, because no one ever has heard of paying as little for carpet as I do.

Getting these great deals has been especially easy for me because I live within driving distance of the "carpet capital of the world," Dalton, Georgia, which is about 90 minutes northwest of Atlanta. But people in Dalton tell me that I'm far from alone. Most of their business now comes from people who order carpet from a store in Dalton and have it shipped to them. Usually, these long-distance customers will order a specific brand and style of carpet, trying to get it at a lower price than they would pay at home.

But that's not my game. I drive to Dalton and go to any of the many carpet showrooms in the area. Then I look for carpet that nobody wants to talk about: the carpet that's in the unmarked back rooms of the big carpet sellers. In many cases, these carpets are from the beginning or end of the manufacturing run, and the color does not match the sample that's handed out to stores around the country. There's nothing wrong with the color. It just doesn't match the sample.

Buying carpet in this way gets you fantastic markdowns from the normal price of the carpet, sometimes as little as $3 to $6 a yard for carpet that normally sells for $18 to $20 a yard. But if you're going to be shipping your carpet to Chicago, Pittsburgh, or Los Angeles, you have to buy enough carpet—and save enough money—to cover the freight costs. It's really pretty easy to do, according to Jerry Hennon, general manager of one of Dalton's largest carpet stores, Carpets of Dalton (www.carpetsofdalton. com). You can have the carpet shipped to your home, to a freight terminal, or to any business with a loading dock, Hennon said. Having it shipped to your home might not be the best idea, because the truck driver, usually a common carrier, may or may not be helpful. The cost is 35 to 45 cents a yard for shipments to destinations in the Southeast United States, and up to 85 or 95 cents a yard to California. Carpets of Dalton contacts the freight line for you and coordinates the delivery.

How do you know what to buy? The carpet store will ask you what you're interested in, then send you samples to review, Hennon said. That way you'll know whether you like the carpet.

The carpet in most Dalton stores is kept in vast warehouses that contain hundreds of rolls of carpet. The best deals often come from the beginning or the end of a manufacturing run, or the carpet might be irregular because of a defect in the weave. Before you buy, ask the store to unroll the carpet in a well-lit area, and get down on your hands and knees and examine it. A place that we bought from last time has a machine with big lights above it and they unroll the carpet as slow or as fast as you want. It's not as easy as looking at little swatches of carpet, but you get a much better idea how the carpet will look in your home. Just as with paint, it's easier to see if you like the color if you see a ten-foot section of it, rather than a one-inch-square sample. One time there was a carpet I thought I was going to buy, and when they unrolled it, there was a defect, so I didn't buy it. If I hadn't had it unrolled, I wouldn't have known. If you go to a store that won't unroll it, don't buy it.

The salespeople won't spend a lot of time with you if you buy in the back room because they live on commission, and there's no money for them in the back room. That's actually better, because you're free to spend as much time as you want going from carpet to carpet. Make sure to bring a pen and a legal-size pad, so you can make a sketch of where you are in the warehouse and which rolls you like. Otherwise you'll get confused and forget where the ones you like are located and what they cost.

Good-quality carpet depends on the type and quality of the carpet fiber, the weight of the fiber, and the way it is manufactured. Hennon recommends a name-brand nylon carpet, 35 to 40 ounces and up in weight, that has a good twist to it. If you look closely at the carpet fibers, the tips should have a sharp, pencil-point appearance. That means it's been properly twisted. Poorly made carpet will have very little twist and the tips will have a frayed look. Quality carpet should look good for five to ten years, but cheap carpet can look ugly in as little as six months.

Good padding and proper installation are very important to the look and wear of the carpet. Hennon recommends $\frac{7}{16}$-inch, eight-pound or better padding, especially for high-traffic areas. Installation will cost $4.50 to $5.50 a square yard, more for stairs or things like moving furniture or removing existing carpet. You can find an industry-certified installer at www.cfi-installers.org.

With some of the carpets I've bought, the installation has been more expensive than the carpet. I'm paying about $4 a yard for delivery and installation, and more for the padding.

It makes sense to carpet several rooms at a time, so you can spread out the delivery cost. But one mistake people make is that they buy a ton of the same carpet and put it throughout their house. That doesn't look as good as using a different carpet, and creating an individual look, in each room. One of the advantages of buying in Dalton in these "remnant rooms" is there isn't enough of any one kind to carpet an entire floor of the house.

If you choose to buy carpet from a store near your home, your best bet is to shop at Home Depot and Costco, who are challenging the carpet industry and putting enormous pricing pressure on it. As the No. 2 and No. 5 retailers in the country, they can live with much lower markups and they have decided to move into a business that has been dominated by independent retailers. It's had an enormous effect.

The price of carpet can be confusing, because you'll see it listed as the price per square yard or the price per square foot, depending on the store. Sometimes both prices will be listed. The carpet industry started switching to the per-square-foot prices because hardwood, stone, and tile all were being quoted by the square foot. To minimize confusion, the carpet industry started switching to square-foot pricing. Carpet prices of $15 to $20 a square yard were looking expensive, at a glance, compared to hardwood flooring, which might cost $5 a square foot. In reality, carpet at $18 a square yard actually is $2 a square foot (because there are nine square feet in a square yard), and hardwood that's $5 a square foot really costs $45 a square yard. To make the conversion, multiply the square-foot price by nine, or divide the square-yard price by nine.

One of the interesting things Home

Depot has done—and I like it—is to quote a price for carpet, pad, and installation, all at one price per square foot. For the consumer, it means there's one easy price you can use to compare, instead of having to add the cost of the carpet, pad, installation, and delivery. And there's one party who is responsible for the installation of the carpet. Most of the problems people have with carpet come from installation, when the carpet isn't properly stretched into place. It ends up looking rumpled, and wears poorly.

Flooring can be expensive, and you should use your neighborhood as a guideline for the decisions you make. People pay for a house based on selling prices in your neighborhood, and if you over-improve your house, when you sell it, you'll never get back anything close to the money you spent on the improvements. So if people in your neighborhood have vinyl floors in the bathrooms, you shouldn't tile your bathroom floor—unless you're doing it for your own enjoyment. If people have hardwood floors in the kitchen and carpet everywhere else, you shouldn't do hardwood floors throughout the house, unless you prefer hardwood.

If you have an older-style home, from the era when people covered up hardwood floors with carpet, there's tremendous value in pulling up the carpet and refinishing the hardwood floors, because people put such a premium on hardwood floors today. I've owned houses that were built in 1937, 1939, and 1947, and all had hardwood everywhere.

If you add hardwood floors to your home, you'll have three basic choices: laminate flooring, "engineered" flooring, and solid wood flooring. Laminate, which most people know by the brand name Pergo, looks like hardwood but isn't wood at all. It's made of a countertop-like material, like Formica, that has an image of wood on the surface. An engineered floor has one layer or more of wood on the surface and several more layers below, kind of like plywood. Solid wood is just what it sounds like: It consists of wood planks, usually ¾ inch in thickness, and from 1½ to 8 inches in width. Most solid wood floors are red or white oak, but there are several other varieties, including maple, cypress, and cherry.

Laminate, as you might expect, is cheaper. Next is an engineered floor, and solid wood is the most expensive. For a typical two-room, 400-square-foot job, expect to pay about $2,000 for laminate, $2,500 for an engineered floor, and $2,600 for solid wood, including installation.

If you're adding the floor over a concrete surface, the best choices are laminate or an engineered floor, according to Brian Butler, owner of Butler Hardwood Floor Inc. Because solid wood is nailed into place, there's a chance the planks would come up if installed over concrete. Laminate is installed over a foam pad and its joints snap together or are glued. An engineered floor is usually glued down. So both are more stable over concrete.

If you're adding the floor over another surface, solid wood is a good choice because of its long life—you can refinish it again and again.

If you're capable of installing hard-wood floors yourself, you can cut the cost of adding hardwood substantially. Laminate costs about $3 a square foot for the material, or about $1,200 for 400 square feet. A home-improvement store might charge you another $2 a square foot to install it. An engineered floor might be $3.75 a square foot for the prefinished flooring and glue, plus $2.50 a square foot to install. Solid wood might be $2 a square foot for the unfinished wood, $2 a square foot for installation, and $2.50 a square foot to sand and finish the floor.

Costco sells a kit that has everything you need. But you have to know yourself. I couldn't do it if there was a firing squad waiting for me.

If, like most of us, you need help, you can find someone in your area who sells and installs the flooring at the Web site of the National Wood Flooring Association (www.woodfloors.org). Butler says you should make sure the installer follows the standards and procedures of the Wood Flooring Manufacturers Association (NOFMA), such as sanding a solid wood floor three times for a smoother surface. Ask them, "How many times are you going to cut (sand) the floor?" And ask to see the work they did at their last job.

One more thing you should know about solid wood flooring is that it comes in different grades. The standard is called "No. 1 common." The wood planks will have a few knot holes and dark mineral streaks. Just above that in quality is "select and better." It costs about $1 a square foot more, and has a more uniform appearance and almost no knot holes. Still higher in quality is "clear," which is extremely uniform, with no knot holes or mineral streaks. The cost is about $1.25 above select and better, or $2.25 a square foot above No. 1 common. So for a 400-square-foot job, add $400 for select and better, $900 for clear. Below the quality scale from No. 1 common is No. 2 common. You would save about 35 cents a square foot for flooring that Butler says is very knotty with a lot of variation.

Tile and stone are two other popular choices in flooring. People often use stone in a foyer, tile in a kitchen, bathroom, laundry room, or sunroom. While hardwood has become more and more popular in kitchens, it's not as water-resistant as tile. So if the dishwasher ever overflows when you're not home, water can get under the hardwood and cause damage.

Tile isn't waterproof either; it's water resistant. When it is installed in a shower, a special pan liner goes under the floor and tar paper goes behind the gypsum-board walls to make it waterproof, according to Joshua Bowden, a tile installation contractor and owner of J.B. Design Tile and Stone. For floors, a waterproof membrane must be installed. If tile is installed over a concrete floor, the installer must use an antifracture membrane, otherwise the tile eventually will crack.

Tile is even more expensive per square foot than hardwood, although the average job usually is smaller. Bowden said his typical job is a 100-square-foot to 300-square-foot kitchen, a master bathroom of 150 to 200 square feet, or a small bathroom of 50 to 60 square feet. At about $7 a square foot installed, it would cost $1,400 for a 200-square-foot job, installed. Marble or limestone, popular flooring materials, could cost $2.50 more a square foot.

Installers charge more for more intricate patterns, perhaps $1 a square foot more for a diagonal pattern, and more to remove old tile. Bowden said it could cost $5 a square foot to have old tile removed and hauled away.

• Tips on Carpet and Flooring •

○ Consider ordering carpet from a store in Dalton, Georgia, where most carpet is manufactured, and having it shipped to your home.

○ If you choose to buy carpet from a store locally, your best bet is to shop at Home Depot and Costco, which are putting enormous pressure on the industry to lower prices.

○ Consider wood floors if you prefer wood, but not to increase the value of your home.

○ There are three kinds of "wood" floors: Laminate, engineered, and solid wood. Solid wood lasts the longest but is the most expensive. Laminate and engineered floors work best when installed over concrete floors.

○ Tile and stone are more expensive than hardwood. Tile costs about $7 a square foot installed.

• Internet •

www.carpetsofdalton.com

www.cfi-installers.org

www.woodfloors.org   (National Wood Flooring Association)

www.nofma.org   (The Wood Flooring Manufacturers Association)

✳ SHEETS AND TOWELS ✳

The best way to save money on housewares, such as sheets, blankets, and towels, is to buy irregulars. You can save a fortune.

One of the best places to buy these items is Value City, which has irregulars of just about any houseware item. Irregular sheets might have a minor stitching error—but who's going to notice? I don't, and I make a bed with hospital corners, something I picked up at a camp where you had to be able to bounce a quarter off your bed. It drives my wife crazy.

I've bought beautiful king-size blankets for $19 that would have cost $90 to $100 or more if they were first quality.

The most dramatic savings for sheet sets are for the premium, very-high-thread-count sheets, because most people who buy ultra-premium sheets aren't interested in irregulars. These sheets are very comfortable, and when you buy irregulars, all you'll notice are that they're the best sheets you've ever had, and the price was great—as little as $30 for a queen set. That's probably less than an inferior set of first-quality sheets would cost.

More and more, stores are advertising the thread counts of linens, which technically are the number of threads running vertically and horizontally in one square inch of fabric. The most common style of sheets, percale, have a thread count of 180–200. Luxury sheets these days have thread counts of 300 and above, some even higher than 600. But you can't judge a sheet just by its thread count or by the use of premium cottons such as Egyptian, pima, and supima, because the fit of the sheets and the strength and durability of the fabric—not just the softness—also are factors. If you can get a quality sheet set for a good price, that's all you have to worry about.

If you like ultra-premium sheets, blankets, and towels, or want to give them a try, a great option is Tuesday Morning, which sells extremely high quality brand names at very good prices, but more money than I would pay. Tuesday Morning says it sells closeout merchandise at 50 percent to 80 percent off the prices you'd see in a department store or upscale catalog. They're not open all the time, but more than they used to be. When I checked, Tuesday Morning said its stores were open from Feb. 5 to March 30, April 16 to June 30, Aug. 6 to Sept. 30, and Oct. 1 to Dec. 31. Check www.tuesday morning.com for details.

A couple of good sites to check are www.smartbargains.com, which lets you buy online, and www.overstock.com, an online liquidator.

Sometimes you'll find a deal just because the color is being discontinued. We saw some huge, oversize bath towels at Costco for $6.99, but there was one color, a shade of blue, that was on sale for $2.77 (closeouts at Costco always end in 77 cents. At Sam's Club, they end in 91 cents). The new blue color was right next to it, and it was $6.99.

• Tips on Sheets and Towels •

❍ Buy irregulars for huge savings.

❍ Check Value City and Tuesday Morning for excellent deals, especially on premium goods.

• Internet •

www.smartbargains.com
www.overstock.com

✳ HIGH-EFFICIENCY LIGHTBULBS ✳

My wife and I had been in a constant war over the lighting in our home, but we finally reached a compromise. I was changing all the lightbulbs, removing regular incandescent lightbulbs and replacing them with energy-efficient compact fluorescent bulbs. Then Lane would replace the compact fluorescents with regular bulbs. She didn't like the light from the low-energy bulbs, which is whiter rather than yellowish—more like the light in an office building.

Our compromise was that I get to put in whatever bulb I want overhead, and Lane gets to control the lamps. So now, as a traditional bulb burns out in the overhead fixtures, I replace it with a high-efficiency bulb, and the cost of lighting our home goes down and down. The compact fluorescents use about one-fourth the electricity of traditional bulbs.

If you tried using compact fluores-cents a few years ago, try again, because the light they provide is much better than it used to be, more like that of in-candescent bulbs. The price, while still higher than regular bulbs, has come down dramatically. Compact fluores-cents used to cost $15 to $20 each. Today they're $3.50 to $4 each, and they last for years. Still, it's hard to convince people, when they can buy lightbulbs on sale for 25 cents each, to pay $4. But the cost of the bulb is insignificant compared to the cost of the electricity it uses, and tradi-tional incandescent bulbs are terribly in-efficient in how they use electricity. For every $1 you spend on electricity with an incandescent, you get about 10 cents worth of light and 90 cents worth of heat, according to Southface Energy In-stitute (www.southface.org). Over the life of a compact fluorescent bulb, you'll save $30 to $40 in energy costs. You won't see the savings on your electric bill, because lights are a relatively small energy user compared to your refrigerator and air conditioner. But over time, making these changes will have an effect.

Our kitchen, for example, has ten can-style spotlights, and nine of them have compact fluorescent bulbs. I'm waiting for the tenth to burn out.

Outdoor floodlights are an even better deal, because the price difference between regular bulbs and compact fluorescents is minimal, perhaps $5 versus $4 for a regular bulb, and compact fluorescents use less energy and last longer.

Compact fluorescents now come in all shapes and styles. I buy them at Costco, but they're available everywhere. Southface recommends looking for bulbs with a Color Rendering Index (CRI) of 80 or higher, for the best light quality.

If you're looking for other ways to cut your monthly electricity usage, there are two ways to make a big difference. First, check the insulation in your attic. If it looks light, see if your electric or gas company will do a home energy audit, or get an estimate from companies that will blow in additional insulation or add sheets of insulation, called batting. Increasing insulation can pay for itself in as little as two seasons. Second, if your house is usually empty while you're at work, have a programmable thermostat installed. They enable you to raise the temperature in the summer when you're at work, but cool the house down before you get home, and vice versa in the winter.

• Tips on High-Efficiency Lightbulbs •

○ Compact fluorescents provide better light, more like that of traditional lightbulbs, and are much cheaper than they were a few years ago.

○ Compact fluorescents now come in virtually all shapes and sizes.

○ A compact fluorescent bulb can last ten times as long as a regular incandescent bulb, and a single bulb can save you $30 to $40 in energy costs over its lifetime.

• Internet •

www.southface.org

✳ SMOKE DETECTORS ✳

If you have a burglar alarm in your house, make sure you have a smoke alarm that's integrated into the burglar alarm system. That will give you whole-house protection, and you'll never have to worry about it.

If you don't have a burglar alarm, and you don't want to go to that expense, you can buy a relatively new style of smoke alarm that provides great protection at a great price. The new smoke alarms use a lithium battery that lasts for ten years. That's a much better choice than the old-style smoke detectors whose batteries must be replaced once or twice a year. Firefighters say that people die in fires when there are no smoke detectors or when the smoke detectors aren't working, either because someone has disabled them or because the batteries are dead.

The ten-year smoke detectors are so cheap now—routinely less than $10—that you can put them throughout your house. It's a very inexpensive form of life insurance. Write the date you installed them on or near the smoke detector, so you'll know when to replace the battery.

People have the most trouble with a smoke detector in the kitchen. That's the one people tend to disable, because it's accidentally triggered by a dinner gone awry. I recommend placing one near the kitchen, in the laundry room, and in each bedroom.

The laundry room is something people don't think about much, but it's a prime location for a fire to start. The clothes dryer is the source of some of the most dreadful fires to ever hit a home. People often forget to clean the lint screen in their dryer, or the exhaust pipe that carries the hot air outside their house. Lint clogs trap heat, and the lint is like kindling for a fire. Within a couple of minutes, a fire can reach more than 1,000 degrees. Many people also store things around a dryer that can catch fire. When I learned about this I went and looked at our dryer, and we had boxes and papers next to it. We were setting ourselves up for a tremendous possibility of a fire. Now we've cleaned all of that out.

If you have the old kind of smoke detectors, throw them out and buy the ten-year kind. There are times when it pays to be cheap and there are times when it doesn't pay to be cheap. It doesn't pay to be cheap with smoke detectors.

Another great way to protect your house from fire is to buy fire extinguishers. There are different extinguishers for different types of fires. For example, Class A fire extinguishers are for ordinary combustibles such as wood and paper, and Class B fire extinguishers are for flammable liquids, mainly grease and gasoline. Class C fire extinguishers are for electrical fires and Class D fire extinguishers are for combustible metals. So you probably should keep a Class B fire extinguisher in your kitchen, where a grease fire is more likely. Some extinguishers have multiple ratings. I just bought a First Alert fire extinguisher at Costco that is rated for Class A, B, and C fires for $18. If you can find one that is rated for several different kinds of fires, that's great. Costco also had Kidde brand extinguishers for a similar price. Either would be fine.

Keep one fire extinguisher in the laundry room and one in the kitchen, at least.

Mark Meltzer had to put out a fire with a fire extinguisher shortly after he moved into his house. An old condensate pump on his air conditioner seized and caught fire. Mark noticed that the air conditioning had stopped, went to the basement to check, and found flames coming from the tiny pump, just a few feet from a gas line leading to his water heater. He grabbed a fire extinguisher, which he had in the basement, and put out the fire. Then he called the fire department, which cut out the pump, eliminating any danger that it would smolder and reignite. If Mark had had no fire extinguisher handy, the fire could have been disastrous.

You can be overcome with smoke very quickly. If you have a fire in your house and it's getting big, get out. Don't try to save anything but yourself and your family.

• Tips on Smoke Detectors •

○ If you have a burglar alarm in your house, get a smoke alarm that's integrated into the burglar alarm system.

○ If you don't have a burglar alarm, throw out your old smoke detectors and install the new lithium battery-powered smoke detectors that last for ten years. They cost less than $10 each.

○ Clean the lint screen and exhaust pipe for your clothes dryer, and move papers away from it. The dryer is a prime place for fires to start.

○ Keep fire extinguishers in your laundry room and kitchen.

✳ FURNITURE ✳

The furniture business always has been controlled by local or regional chains, and people generally have purchased their furniture from one of a few stores that advertise heavily in their area. But now consumers have the ability to price shop, via the Internet, furniture sold by retailers who are reaching outside their traditional market, and that's making an enormous difference. One such retailer, the largest in the nation, is Warren Buffett's Nebraska Furniture Mart (www.nebraskafurnituremart.com). Another is Gallery Furniture (www.gallery furniture.com) in Houston.

More and more, instead of buying from a furniture retailer a few minutes from home, people are driving as long as a day to a high-volume furniture outlet. Nebraska Furniture Mart has become famous in Omaha and is opening a second location in Kansas City, where people across the Midwest buy furniture at what they perceive to be really good prices. Another furniture seller that's become a magnet for shoppers is IKEA, which sells Scandinavian-style furniture at low prices. IKEA stores are mostly on the East and West coasts of the United States. You can find a list of IKEA store locations at www.ikea.com, but you can't buy online, and the site isn't very friendly or navigable.

So many people drive great distances to shop at IKEA that it's not unusual to find a number of new motels near IKEA stores. People show up with trucks, spend the night, and start shopping at IKEA the next morning. They load up the truck and take their furniture home. IKEA also has a mail-order program, but it's not cost-competitive with IKEA stores.

Costco is expanding its role in furniture sales. It's opening a furniture store called Furniture Only in the Pacific Northwest, and selling more and more furniture (including upholstered furniture) in all its stores. Costco has two primary furniture events a year: one that starts just before Christmas, and another in mid-July. And the furniture Costco sells is a tremendous deal—excellent quality at very low prices. Costco marks up its furniture no more than 9 percent above its cost, compared to the 100 percent markup you'll find at most furniture stores. If Costco pays $500 for a piece, it sells for $545 instead of the $1,000 a traditional furniture store would charge. We have Costco furniture throughout our house.

Costco doesn't deliver it for you, but at those prices, you can afford to rent a truck and pick it up. You buy it and Costco sets it aside for you. Then you rent a truck and take it home. During the furniture events, there's an area near the pharmacy where you see piece after piece of sold furniture waiting to be picked up.

Another thing you won't find at Costco is what I call No-No-No plans. Those are the financing plans furniture stores use to drive most furniture sales. Furniture stores don't advertise the quality of their furniture, just their No-No-No plans, which means they charge no interest, no down payment, and no payments until January two years from now. People have become completely obsessed with these plans, and the idea of furnishing an entire room or an entire house without having to pay for it. Buyers think it's free money, but the reality is No-No-No plans can be dangerously expensive, because people often

fail to pay in full before the date that the No-No-No payment holiday ends. If you don't pay in full by the day the grace period ends, you get clobbered. The store charges you interest retroactive on the entire balance to the day of purchase—usually at an interest rate of 20 percent or more. That would be a staggering amount of money. If you buy something on a No-No-No plan and you are nearing the date to pay in full, and you can't make the payment, you should do anything you have to to come up with the money. I don't care if you have to take a cash advance on your credit card. One of the tricks they use is that the payment due date may not match up with the date the No-No-No ends, so you think you've paid it in time, but that could be a week or two after the trigger date. Make sure you keep a record of the actual date your payment holiday ends, and send in your payment by FedEx, UPS, or certified mail, to make sure you get it there in time. Do not trust regular mail with this. Period. No exceptions.

People use these plans because furniture is expensive, and because they want a lot at one time. My philosophy about furniture is different from what is common today. I buy one piece of furniture at a time, rather than a set of furniture. So I might buy a bed or a dresser. Later, I might buy another piece that complements the earlier purchase, but doesn't exactly match it. That's the way people used to buy furniture, and if you look in the home of an older relative, you'll see that the pieces complement each other but don't exactly match. That's also true in high-end homes. The idea of having pieces that all match is a modern one, driven by marketing and the fact that people don't trust themselves to make good choices.

It's much easier to come up with $700 or $800 for one piece of furniture than $7,000 or $8,000 for a set. Instead, people today put themselves deep into debt to buy a room full of furniture.

It's best to buy furniture that you can see and take with you. But sometimes furniture is delivered to you from a warehouse, or people elect to custom-order a piece with a particular fabric. If you aren't going to take the furniture with you, pay by credit card, not by cash, check, or debit card. Furniture stores close all the time, even well-known stores, and if you pay by cash, check, or debit card, you could lose your money and not get your furniture. I've talked with a lot of people over the years who've lost money this way. It happens over and over again. If you pay by credit card and don't receive the merchandise, just do a chargeback within 60 days, and you'll receive a refund from your credit card company.

In the carpet section, I told you about buying carpet inexpensively in Dalton, Georgia, the carpet capital of the world. There's a parallel in furniture: North Carolina, where a lot of furniture is manufactured. The North Carolina furniture stores, because they're close to the manufacturers, can buy furniture for less. But just as with carpet, buying in the back room and finding a one-of-a-kind item will be much cheaper than simply ordering furniture from a North Carolina store.

Unfortunately, over the years I've heard more complaints from listeners who bought furniture in North Carolina than virtually any other consumer purchase that people make. Sometimes I'll hear from someone who bought from a place that went bust or they bought from a place that was supposed to deliver the furniture, but the delivery was delayed. The most common problem is that the furniture shows up damaged, and nobody accepts responsibility. The store says they gave good furniture to the company that delivered the merchandise and the carrier blames the store. It's almost impossible to resolve.

When furniture is damaged on the way to a furniture store, the retailer refuses delivery and the manufacturer doesn't want it back. So it goes to a furniture jobber, which expertly repairs it and puts it up for sale, usually in the jobber's own liquidation facility. You can find furniture jobbers at flea markets, antique stores, and galleries. Ask a dealer at a flea market or the owner of an antique store for names. You might also find scratch-and-dent damaged furniture at the outlet center of a furniture retailer.

A great way to save money on furniture, and we do this all the time, is to buy it used. What we don't buy at Costco or one of the other warehouse clubs, we buy used, and we have more used furniture than anything else. A lot of people are uncomfortable with the idea of buying used furniture, but buying used gives you the chance to save money and buy a much better piece of furniture. Furniture depreciates even faster than a new car when it's driven off the lot, so a used piece is a lot cheaper than new. We furnished our entire five-bedroom beach house in Florida for just $3,000. If you buy used, you might pay $200 for a dresser, $50 for a night stand, $100 for a headboard. Our dining-room table at the beach house was $200, including four chairs.

A lot of cities have furniture antique markets where you can find used furniture once a month. Although they're called antique markets, a lot of the stu is just used. An antique ultima comes a very expensive used piece is just a deal. It's easy to tell the difference. An antique bookcase might cost $4,000, while a used bookcase might cost $75. Our dining-room table at home is magnificent. It's a traditional mahogany table with eight English ball-and-claw chairs. It easily would have cost $10,000 new and we bought it at one of the antique markets for $1,400. That's still a lot of money, but it's such a high-quality piece that it will last for generations.

Another way to buy good used furniture is at estate or moving sales, or from people who are redecorating. Check your local classified ads or free local advertising sheets, which some people know as the *Pennysaver*, to see what's available.

In mountain and beach resort communities, wher⸺ ⸺e are a large number of second homes, there is an abundance of barely used furniture. Someone sells a property and the buyer doesn't want the furniture, so it goes to secondhand furniture shops. It's high-end stuff, because people who can afford to own a second home often have very nice furniture in it. And it sells very inexpensively.

One of the ways furniture stores try to get you to spend more is to sell you fabric protection plans. Don't buy them. In the manufacturing of upholstered furniture, manufacturers treat the fabric with protectant. The furniture store is just trying to pad its profit.

Ordering custom-made furniture also is a bad idea. Anytime you get into custom-made furniture, you create complexity, delays, higher costs, and customer-service problems. That's especially true for sofas.

iture •

⸺ns, buy used furniture or furniture that has been damaged
⸺.

⸺o come from Costco, which has a low markup over its cost,
⸺nal furniture stores such as Nebraska Furniture Mart.

HOME IMPROVEMENT · 171

- Don't use the No-No-No (no interest, no down payment, and no payments until sometime in the future) plans to buy furniture. People often fail to pay in full before the date that the No-No-No payment holiday ends, and they end up getting clobbered—paying 20 percent or more interest, retroactive on the entire balance to the day of purchase.

- Consider buying one piece of furniture at a time, the way affluent people buy furniture, rather than a large set of matching furniture.

• Internet •

www.galleryfurniture.com

www.ikea.com

www.nebraskafurnituremart.com

✻ HOME SERVICES ✻

I love a bargain, but when it comes to hiring someone to work in my home, I put more of a premium on the person, not the price.

I've used the same yard service and the same pool service since I bought my home in 1996. I've used the same plumber since 1998. I've used the same heating and air conditioning company since the early 1990s and I've used the same security system in all the houses I've lived in since 1983. That's a long time.

I try to find service workers I think are good people, then I use them for routine jobs so I can find out if they're reliable, dependable, and know what they're doing. If I like the person and their work on small jobs, I know I can trust them when a major job comes up.

I never want to hire somebody when I'm in a jam, because then I'm vulnerable. The time to ask, "Which plumber should I use?" is not when there's a geyser in your house. My co-author,

Mark Meltzer, came home one Saturday evening to find water gushing into the basement apartment where his father lives. Mark knew how to turn off the main water supply inside the house, but unfortunately that didn't stop the water. It turned out that the main water line from the street had burst, but at a point between where it entered the house and the main water valve. Mark could have stopped the water had he known how to turn off the water valve near the curb, but he didn't. So Mark was trying to suction up the water with a carpet cleaner, but fighting a losing battle. He didn't have a regular plumber, and it was a Saturday night, so finding one was difficult. Eventually he got someone to come to the house and shut off the water, but he called me at home before he got ripped off. The plumber wanted $1,600 to replace the broken pipe and connect a temporary water line to supply water to the house until the pipe was fixed. I told Mark to pay the guy for the service call and say, "No thanks." Instead he got a plumber to replace the pipe for $800 and he set up a temporary water line on his own by hooking a $30 hose to a neighbor's spigot. So he saved hundreds of dollars. Once the crisis was over, he called friends for referrals, and another plumber told him how to set up the temporary water line. So Mark dealt with the catastrophe first, then took his time to find the right quote. If something is outside your own expertise and someone is asking for real money—whether it's a repair to your house or your car or something else—the answer is to get another estimate. The only exception to that is if you're dealing with someone whom you trust thoroughly.

Sometimes what looks like a disaster can turn out okay. We had a water heater that started leaking and needed to be replaced, and when we put in the new water heater, our natural gas bills outside the heating season dropped so much I kept thinking there was a mistake in the bill. The new water heater, nine years ahead of the one it replaced, uses less gas to do the job. A University of Wisconsin report shows that a water heater lasts an average of thirteen years, and recommends that owners replace theirs after ten years, before it dies on its own. The water heater is the second-largest user of energy in the house, after the heating and air conditioning system, and it performs especially poorly in the last few years of its life. Plus, if you re-place it before it fails, you'll be able to shop around and not be in an emer-gency situation. With a water heater, it's worth spending more for higher energy efficiency, rather than buying a cheaper one that's less efficient.

I hear several complaints about the people who work inside your home. One is reliability—they say they're going to come and then they don't come. Or they start out being reliable and you think you've found the answer, but over time, for whatever reason, they become unreliable.

Sometimes you run into trouble be-cause a handyman is good in one area, but not another. Maybe they're good at carpentry but not at painting or electrical work. And they would be doing them-selves and you a favor by telling you that's not their strongest skill. Sometimes people ask me questions that are outside my area of expertise, and I have to have the judgment to tell people that I don't know the answer.

Finding good service people is a trial-and-error process, and the best way to start is to ask friends, neighbors, and co-workers if they have someone they like. I also ask them who they used in the past that they didn't like, so I don't make the mistake of hiring a person or a company that someone else didn't like. Word of mouth helps you learn from other people's trial and error. Using someone that someone else liked doesn't mean you'll like them as well. But it's the best way to begin the search. Mark used a cleaning person someone recommended that did a mediocre job, so he didn't hire them again. And he talked with a handy-man a neighbor recommended who never showed up. If that happens, you just try again.

Sometimes you can find a good service person based on a recommendation from someone at the paint store, the tile store, or the hardware store. But again, it's not foolproof. We hired a tile company based on a recommendation from the tile store, and the people completely butchered the job. The worker quit halfway through, and the contractor had to come in and redo what he had already done. The job was in the master bathroom, and the thing was so messed up that we couldn't live in the master bedroom for six weeks. It should have been a three-day job. The owner probably lost a lot of money on the job, so nobody was happy.

The one way you should never hire someone is from a flier in your mailbox. That's where most of the unreliable people, and the people who are actively trying to rip you off, come from. Over the years in my TV work, when we've done "victim" stories, we've found repeatedly that the dishonest service person knocked on the victim's door or left a flier at the mailbox. Most good people and companies are so

busy that they're not going to be dropping leaflets door by door.

Another thing you shouldn't do is give someone money to buy materials. Most often when someone asks for money to get started, you'll never see them again. But if you're dealing with a contractor who doesn't have the money to front the materials he needs, go with him to the hardware store or wherever he's buying the materials, and buy the materials yourself. That also eliminates another danger: that you might get hit with a lien if the contractor fails to pay for the materials. I had a neighbor who put an addition on his home and did a major renovation of his kitchen, and wound up losing an additional $70,000 because of a contractor who didn't pay his subcontractors.

I'd say getting a referral for a service worker gives you a yellow caution light to proceed, while a flier at the door is a red light. There are no green lights, although time can turn a yellow light into a green light. Each time you have a good experience with a service person, it increases the odds that the next experience also will be good.

Checking references is worthwhile if someone is doing a major job, and if a job could be dangerous, you should check to see if someone has workers' compensation and liability insurance. For example, you may have to hire a tree service to trim trees on your property or cut one down. That's dangerous work, and companies often do not have proper insurance. If a worker gets hurt and they don't have proper insurance, it's your insurance company that's going to have to pay, because the work occurred on your property. If you need some minor tree work and it doesn't involve a lot of climbing, make your own decision on the insurance issue. But if you're hiring someone to take down a large tree, or remove a dead tree, and it looks like a dangerous job, make sure the company has workers' comp and liability insurance. And don't just believe their letter. Talk with their broker or insurance agent to make sure the insurance is current.

Hiring a housekeeper, something that's become increasingly common with the abundance of two-income families, presents the challenge of theft. Rarely are people or companies insured or bonded, and even if they are, it doesn't mean much unless you catch a housekeeper in the act of stealing. There's probably no area where trust is a greater issue, because you're inviting someone into the most intimate areas of your home. Many years ago my sister caught the cleaning lady at her house stealing. It just happened that she was walking into a room while the cleaning lady was taking something. She worked for my sister for a long, long time, and she just burst into tears when confronted over the theft. So my sister let her stay on. She worked a number of years after that and there was never another problem.

People ask if they should use an individual or a company, and it doesn't matter as long as you find one you like and trust.

• Tips on Home Services •

○ Finding good service people is a trial-and-error process. Get recommendations, then try people for routine jobs so you can find out if they're reliable, dependable, and know what they're doing. That's more important than price.

○ Try not to hire somebody when you're in a jam, because then you're vulnerable.

○ Never hire someone who leaves a flier or card in your mailbox. That's where most of the unreliable people, and the people who are actively trying to rip you off, come from.

CHAPTER 8

CARS

In my previous book, *Get Clark Smart,* **I wrote about how to buy a car. In this book, I've focused on what to do once you own the car—how best to protect your investment, although I use the term** *investment* **very loosely, because a car, since it loses value over time, actually is the opposite of an investment. It's a lifestyle choice. But there are decisions we make about our cars that can cost us, perhaps a little, perhaps a lot. If we do regular maintenance to keep our cars running well, that minimizes the cost of repairs and can give us years of affordable extra life from the car. If we handle repairs correctly, it can save hundreds or thousands of dollars.**

I hope you find this section very useful in helping you stretch your car dollar, and maybe even stretch its life.

✳ TIRES ✳

You might not think about buying tires for your car on the Internet, but it can save you a tremendous amount of money, depending on the kind of car you have.

My TV producer, Greg Turchetta, didn't believe that you could save by buying tires online. So we did a TV piece on it, and after our research he went from being a complete skeptic to an absolute believer. He surveyed people about what kind of car they had and what kind of tires they needed, and the price differences were gigantic.

You'll save the most money on the Web if you're buying tires for a luxury vehicle or a performance car. You may not save much if you're buying for a traditional large-production car like the Honda Accord. The more unusual the vehicle, the more you'll save. Always comparison shop, so you'll know a good deal when you see it.

When you buy tires over the Internet, you can have them shipped to your home or to the place you choose to install them. I ordered my tires from Tire Rack (www.tirerack.com), had them shipped to my house, then put them in the trunk and took them to the shop that installed them. These Internet sellers find installers who are willing to make their money only on installation—that's where the real money is in tires anyway. I looked up an installer near my house on Tire Rack's Web site, had the tires installed, and then picked up the car. It's really not any more inconvenient than buying from a tire store, which often will have to order the tire you want. What's the difference between ordering from a tire store or ordering online?

My wife's Acura requires tires with a high-performance V speed rating, and they're quite expensive. But the savings at Tire Rack were shocking. I bought a set of Bridgestone RE88s that were just $78 each, compared to $115 with my buddies at Costco. The installer charged $15 a tire for mounting and balancing. Interestingly, there was less of a price difference with Michelin's high-speed tire, the XGTV4, which was $118 at Tire Rack and $129.99 at Costco. What really stunned me was Tire Rack had a special on another V-rated tire, a Yokohama brand, for just $43 a tire. That's unbelievably cheap for a high-speed-rated tire. I may buy a set and store them for when we need to replace the Bridgestones. The bottom line is you can save by buying online and you can save even more if you're willing to shop around looking for a deal.

It may surprise you to learn that with tires there is no relationship between brand name and quality. So even though Michelin has those great commercials with the baby sitting in a tire, Michelin tires aren't necessarily safer than other brands. For example, the *Wall Street Journal* reported that one type of Michelin tire, the XH4, failed a rigorous test conducted by the National Highway Traffic Safety Administration. The test was designed to see if existing tires could meet proposed new government safety standards. Most of the tires—ten of twelve—would meet the proposed standards, according to a consultant hired by the newspaper.

Consumer Reports tested a wide range of tires for braking, handling, and traction, and found several of the economy tires it tested did nearly as well as premium tires, for up to $40 less per tire. In its rating of tires for cars, for example, it gave high marks to the economy Uniroyal Tiger Paw ASC ($33) for great handling, and to the Kelly Navigator Platinum TE ($55) and the Yokohama Avid Touring ($50) for all-around driving.

It sounds simple, but you have to have the correct tire for your car, and you can't always figure out what that is by looking at the existing tire. Lane's Acura wasn't riding well because it repeatedly had the wrong tires. Make sure you get the right size and speed rating, which you should be able to find on the door jamb, the glove compartment, or the fuel door. If you've ever wondered what those numbers and the ones on the side of the tire mean, here it is: If the tire says something like P195/60R15, that's the size of the tire. The P means it's a passenger-car tire. The first number, in this case 195, is the width of the tire in millimeters. The last number, 15, is the diameter of the wheel in inches. The R means radial-ply construction. The 60 means that the sidewall height is 60 percent of the tire's width. The tire might also say 90H. The 90 stands for the maximum load the tire can carry, in this case 1,312 pounds. The "H" is the speed rating, or the maximum speed the tire can go. H is 130 miles per hour. Other speed ratings are S (112 mph), T (118 mph), V (149 mph), and ZR (150 mph or higher). While it's illegal to drive that fast, *Consumer Reports* says that tires with higher speed ratings handle better at normal highway speeds.

When I buy tires, I look for the tire that is the right size and speed rating—and costs the least. The National Highway Traffic Safety Administration and *Consumer Reports* data tell me that just because a tire is a well-known brand like Michelin, that doesn't mean it's going to be the best tire, or even the safest. In the absence of proof that one tire is safer than another, price is the standard I follow. I don't worry about the tread-wear guarantees, because my experience has never matched the claims. As best as I can tell, that's for marketing.

If your tire is shot and you have to replace it, put on a tire that matches the other three, otherwise the car won't ride right.

It's also important to maintain your tires at the right pressure. That was one of the problems in the huge Firestone recall of SUV tires. *Consumer Reports* says tires can leak air over time. Its tests showed tires lost an average of 4.4 pounds per square inch of pressure over six months. Use a tire gauge to check your tire pressure, when the tires are cold, each month. You'll find the correct pressure on the door jamb or the fuel door.

Don't overinflate either. My co-author, Mark Meltzer, was on a trip to the Northeast one winter and stayed overnight in a motel. It was very cold out, and in the morning, he noticed that one tire looked low. He added air without checking the pressure, and when he got back on the road, the overinflated tire heated up and the pressure grew, causing a blowout. Mark had to put the limited-service spare on in the middle of a snowy median, then buy a new pair of rear tires. It made for a very unpleasant road trip.

Other things to keep an eye out for, according to *Consumer Reports*, are uneven wear, which could mean poor alignment, brakes, or shock absorbers; and tires that have cuts, bubbles, or bulges, "which could mean failure is imminent."

If you don't buy your tires on the Internet, the places to turn for the lowest prices are the warehouse clubs. There are some drawbacks, though. They have a very limited selection compared to traditional tire stores, and wait times can be frustrating. People often line up at the warehouse stores on weekends before they open, then rush to the tire counter to beat the other customers. Within minutes, wait times can soar. But the prices are excellent. I solve the problem of long waits by leaving the car and picking it up later, rather than waiting in the store for the tires to be installed. I don't want to turn a year older waiting for tires to be installed.

When you shop for tires, always ask for the "drive-out price," because the cost of the tire is only one component of the purchase. There's also the cost of mounting and balancing the tires, which can be vary tremendously from one place to another, and there may be other charges. So you could find that a tire costs $49 at one shop and $59 at another, but the final price is more expensive at the shop that charges $49.

Costco and Sam's Club charge around $7 a tire for mounting and balancing, or $28 for four tires. Other tire shops can charge as much as $18 a tire, or $72 for four tires. That's a lot of money.

The tire business is dominated by regional stores that advertise heavily in their areas. There's no way these chains can win on price, but they can win by offering faster service or other services. Some shops will repair your damaged tire for free, even if you didn't buy it there. You can just walk in off the street and they'll fix it. It's a marketing gimmick. They're hoping that when you buy tires next time, you'll remember how nice they were to you.

• Tips on Tires •

○ Consider buying tires on the Internet for potentially great savings.

○ If you don't buy on the Internet, the places to turn for the lowest prices are the warehouse clubs.

○ Government and *Consumer Reports* tests show that premium brand-name tires are not necessarily the best in quality.

○ Buy the correct tires for your car. The right size and speed rating should be on the door jamb, the glove compartment, or the fuel door.

○ Check your tire pressure monthly when your tires are cold.

• Internet •

www.tirerack.com
www.consumerreports.org

* DETAILING *

You might be surprised to hear me say this, but I think detailing a car is one of the smartest things somebody can do. Spending $60 to $100 to have a car thoroughly cleaned up may seem frivolous, but I don't think it's a waste at all.

We get rid of our cars because we're bored with them, not because the car is no good anymore. If you treat yourself once a year to having your car thoroughly detailed—shampooed and polished inside and out—you'll drive off with your car looking almost as good as it did when you first got into it. It makes people feel great. If detailing makes you fall in love with your car all over again, you'll keep it longer and avoid expensive payments for a new car.

It's kind of like getting all dressed up and going on a nice date with your spouse every so often. It puts the zing back into the relationship.

Now, some people overdo it, and have their car detailed once a month or more. That does seem wasteful. But if you do it once or twice a year, that's perfect.

If you have a leased car, make sure to have the car thoroughly detailed before you turn it in at the end of the lease. If there's anything broken, get it fixed. And take pictures of the car, so you can prove you returned it in excellent condition.

There's no good way to know if a detailing shop does a good job. Ask friends or co-workers who they use. If you like the job a place does, use them again the next time. Otherwise keep searching until you find one you like.

As far as routine washes, the automatic car wash is fine. I go through automatic washes because they're so cheap, but my wife, Lane, gets upset with me because she thinks it's harmful to the car. A lot of people agree with her, but it isn't true. We called ten auto repair and painting shops, and the consensus was they don't see much damage from car washes. Occasionally an antenna breaks or a mirror is broken. A couple of car models reportedly have had design problems that have made them susceptible to such damage. But paint problems are rare and occur mostly with older cars, when the paint is starting to peel anyway and the pressure from the car wash is too great, or on cars that have a manufacturing defect in the paint. Every one of these experts said they take their own cars to an automatic car wash.

• Tips on Detailing •

○ It's a good idea to have your car thoroughly cleaned once or twice a year, well worth the $60 to $100 it costs.

○ If you have a leased car, make sure to have the car thoroughly detailed before you turn it in at the end of the lease.

○ Experts say an automatic car wash is fine for routine washes.

✳ OIL CHANGES ✳

I don't think there's anything I've done in the last few years that caused more controversy than a TV piece I did about how often you should change the oil in your car.

I am not a mechanic, but the oil change business lives on getting you to change your oil more frequently than you need to change it. The truth is, it's absolutely fine, barring some kind of unusual driving pattern, to change your oil only as much as required in the owner's manual for your car. The manufacturer's specifications may call for you to change the oil every 5,000 miles, every 7,500 miles, maybe every 10,000 miles. It depends on the car. But those are the three most common numbers. If your owner's manual says to change your oil every 7,500 miles, that's what your car needs.

The oil-change industry was furious at me for the story I did. Industry people said I was ignoring several factors: that many people drive in harsher-than-average conditions, such as lots of stop-and-go driving or a lot of short trips, which don't allow your car a chance to get warmed up; and that some people drive in very dusty areas. Under such conditions, they say, you should change your oil more frequently than the manufacturer recommends. They also say that, because most people now fill their gas tank themselves, few actually check their oil when they fill up. The argument is that if people don't change their oil for 7,500 miles and don't check their oil, their car might lose oil over time, and their engine might end up with no oil, which would destroy it.

But that's nothing more than a scare tactic. Most cars today don't burn or leak oil, so the danger of burning up your engine is remote. But here's the book answer on how to make sure that doesn't happen. Every other time you fill up your gas tank, check the dipstick to see if the oil level is okay. If you notice a few drops of oil where you park your car, in your garage or at work, you definitely should check the dipstick every other time you fill up. If your car has a minor oil leak, you may have to add oil between oil changes.

Even if you're changing your oil as often as the oil-change places want you to, which is every ten minutes, act immediately if the oil light on your car ever comes on. Pull off the road and stop right away. Do not try to drive to the nearest gas station. They call them "idiot lights" because you're not sup-/posed to ignore them.

For most people, there's absolutely no benefit to changing your oil more often than the manufacturer recommends. You're just wasting money, and if you drive 15,000 miles a year, that could be the difference between two oil changes and five. At $20 a pop, you could save, or waste, about $60.

I take my car in for a routine checkup every 15,000 miles, including an oil change. In the intervening cycle, because my car needs to have the oil changed every 7,500 miles, I go to one of the independent oil-change places. I go to the same one every time, so that if there's ever a question, they can't point fingers. And because I take my car in to my regular service center, I don't buy any costly extras—like getting the coolant changed or windshield wipers replaced—at the oil-change place.

Don't rely on the oil-change place to tell you what oil your car needs. It takes two seconds to look in that owner's manual and see what oil should run in your car. Tell the oil-change place what to use. For example, my hybrid gas/electric car takes "0W," which is a very rare kind of oil. Most cars use 10W or 5W oil. Usually it's 10W40 or 5W40. The 40 means it's for hot weather conditions, while 30 would be more likely for a winter oil change.

People used to change their own oil, but not many do it anymore. Disposing of the oil is one problem, and the space is so tight under the hood in a lot of cars that it's harder for people to get to the oil filter.

• Tips on Oil Changes •

○ Don't change your oil more frequently than your owner's manual says you should.

○ Every other time you fill up your gas tank, check the dipstick to see if the oil level is okay.

○ Get your routine maintenance done by a mechanic once a year. If you go to an oil-change place for oil changes, don't buy any of the extra services, like getting the coolant changed or windshield wipers replaced.

* REPAIRS *

Unless you're a mechanic, taking your car in to be serviced or repaired can be scary. A lot of people worry that an auto repair shop will rip them off. That's why it's important to find a mechanic who knows what he's doing and treats you fairly.

I've been using the same auto repair shop since 1987. My father-in-law, who uses the same shop, feels even more strongly about their work. Believe it or not, when he went shopping recently for a new car, he refused to consider buying any car other than a Honda or Acura—the brands this shop specializes in repairing. He didn't want to deal with the unknown of having his car repaired somewhere else. The mechanic's name is Gordon, so we call that the Gordon Rule.

Many independent shops specialize in fixing certain brands of cars, and this is true especially with the Japanese and European brands, which represent a big chunk of the car market. Normally you get to talk directly with the mechanic who'll be doing the work on your car. That's much better than the system at a typical dealership, where you talk to a service writer who then has to relay to the mechanic your comments about what's wrong with your car. It's easy for something to get lost in the translation. You may not necessarily pay less at one of these independent specialty shops than you do at a dealer, but with car repair price isn't as important as finding someone who is honest and knowledgeable.

The time to find the right mechanic to repair a car is before it's broken. Start by asking people who have your brand of car. Every time you see somebody who's in your "club"—because having a foreign car is like being in a club—ask them how they like it, how it's been running, and where they get their maintenance and repairs done. If you hear the same place mentioned a couple of times, go in there for regular maintenance, a low-risk way to get acquainted. Over time, you can build up trust in their work. This is going to sound shocking, but I trust Gordon so much that when I take my Honda in for a repair, I don't even ask for an estimate, because I know he's not going to pull any stunts on me. He's the real thing.

If you haven't established that kind of relationship, it's critical to get the mechanic's estimate of what's wrong. If the proposed repairs are significant, take the car to another shop for a second opinion, even if you have to have it towed to the second shop. If the estimate is for more than $2,000, it's worth getting two additional estimates.

Having your car towed to another shop for a second opinion may sound extreme, but the cost of a tow is insignificant compared to the hundreds of extra dollars you might pay if the first mechanic is wrong, or is trying to take your money. In my TV work we did a series on auto repair, and we found a woman who had been told her car needed $5,500 in engine and transmission work. The car wasn't driveable, so she had it towed to another repair shop. The second shop diagnosed the problem as a broken tim-ing belt, plus some transmission damage that could be repaired. She paid $1,500, and her car ran great. So by paying for a tow and getting a second opinion, she saved $4,000.

Another woman had a car that was "skipping and popping," which she thought might be a fuel system problem. She took it to a mechanic who had been recommended by friends, and he said the car needed a new clutch, a tune-up, and a fuel filter. She paid $600 to have that work done, $500 of it for the clutch, but when she picked up the car, it still had the original problem. The mechanic then said it needed a new catalytic converter, which would cost $250. She didn't trust him anymore, so she took it to a muffler shop, which said it didn't need a catalytic converter, but it did need a new coil pack. She paid $68 for that, and the muffler shop also adjusted a spark plug wire. The car ran fine for a month, then started skipping and popping again. So she took it back to the muffler shop, which by then had hired a mechanic. He wanted $45 to put the car on a diagnostic machine, and said it did need a catalytic converter and a muffler—and it still needed a fuel filter, which the first mechanic charged her for but never installed. The second mechanic installed the fuel filter and did the diagnostic and charged $90. The car continued to skip and pop. The car's owner then bought a catalytic converter and a muffler from an auto parts store, for another $85, and her brother-in-law installed them. The car still skipped and popped. Finally, the brother-in-law bought some new spark plug wires for $8 and installed them, and that took care of the problem. She had paid $851 and taken the car to three different people to repair a problem that was caused by $8 worth of spark plug wires. She probably needed the new muffler and catalytic converter, but she didn't need the $500 clutch. And all of it could have been avoided if she'd gotten esti-mates from two or three mechanics before she paid for any work.

One of the most important things you can do to keep your car running well is to have regular maintenance done, and make sure to keep your maintenance records. I'm surprised again and again by people who think the only thing you have to do when you own a car is to put gas in and change the oil occasionally. That's not enough. You have to follow the manufacturer's maintenance schedule. It's not there just as advice. It's mandatory. Following it doesn't mean your car will run well, but it sure improves the odds. We keep our cars so much longer now than we used to keep them. The average car on the road in 2001 was 9.3 years old, according to the Car Care Council, a nonprofit organization based in Maryland. Putting some money into maintaining your car is a lot cheaper than new car payments.

• Tips on Repairs •

o Find the right mechanic to repair your car before it's broken. Start by asking people who have your brand of car.

○ Get the mechanic's estimate of what's wrong. If the proposed repairs are significant, take the car to another shop for a second opinion, even if you have to have it towed to the second shop.

○ Keep your car running well by having regular maintenance done.

✳ TOWING ✳

The Automobile Club of America, which everybody knows as AAA, used to have a hammerlock on the towing business, because AAA offered such an all-encompassing service, with tour books, maps, and special trip maps called TripTiks. But now you can plan your driving route using Internet services such as Mapquest (www.mapquest.com) or software such as Delorme's Street Atlas and Microsoft's Streets & Trips. Some cars even use Global Positioning System (GPS) devices to plan your route.

The best way to evaluate AAA is to compare its emergency road service to what others offer. When you do that, AAA, at $35 to $80 a year, doesn't look as good.

Many car insurers now include an emergency road service rider that's very inexpensive. State Farm, for example, has a rider that costs just $2 to $6 a year. It provides a reimbursement for up to $65 if you need to have your car towed, and pays for one hour of labor if you lock your keys in your car, need a jump start, have a flat tire, or run out of gas.

The warehouse clubs also offer emergency road service. Costco's costs just $29.99 a year. The program at Sam's Club comes free when you sign up for the club's $100-a-year "Elite" membership. Both dispatch help for the same list of roadside emergencies. Sam's service comes from the United States Auto Club, Costco's from Road America.

You may also get roadside assistance from your car manufacturer. Many car companies now provide free emergency road service for a year or two, then try to get you to pay for it after that. Compare prices to see if it's worthwhile.

The types of programs are different. AAA and the warehouse clubs dispatch their own trucks to help you, while others allow you to use whatever towing service you wish, then reimburse you by a certain amount per tow. In some ways, the single-fleet service originated by AAA is more convenient, because you don't have to figure out who to call. But the biggest complaint I hear about AAA is how long people have had to wait for the tow truck to arrive. If you use a reimbursement service, keep the name and number of your mechanic or a local towing service with you in your wallet or glove compartment, or as a saved number in your cell phone.

Should you pay $30 to $80 a year for emergency road service? Probably not. How many times in the past five years have you needed a vehicle towed, or needed emergency road service for any other purpose, such as running out of gas or locking your keys in your car? Most people would say never or once. If that's the case, you're better off saving the $150 to $400 you would have spent over those five years and paying the cost of the help out of your pocket when you need it. If you're accident-prone, maybe you should have it. Check with your auto insurer to see what it offers.

If you travel frequently, AAA offers discounts on hotels, car rentals, and cruises that may make it worthwhile. I have remained a AAA member for that reason. You also get the very detailed maps of states and cities that I still find superior to online or computer-based services.

• Tips on Towing •

○ You can buy emergency road service plans from AAA, Costco, Sam's Club, or your insurer.

❍ The types of programs are different. AAA and the warehouse clubs dispatch their own trucks to help you, while others allow you to use whatever towing service you wish, then reimburse you.

❍ If you use a reimbursed plan or no emergency road service plan, keep the number of a local towing service or mechanic with you, in your glove compartment, or in your cell phone.

• Internet •

www.mapquest.com

www.aaa.com

www.costco.com

www.samsclub.com

✳ GASOLINE ✳

The price of gasoline is heading down, and it has nothing to do with world oil supplies or the OPEC oil cartel.

Discounters—led by supermarkets and warehouse clubs Costco and Sam's Club—are gaining a larger foothold in the marketplace and they're starting to put pressure on the major gas retailers. According to the *Wall Street Journal*, mass merchants and grocers such as Kroger already have 15 percent of the gasoline market in the Dallas-Fort Worth area. They were No. 2 in that market and No. 3 in Houston with more than 14 percent of the market. Experts believe that by 2005, non-traditional gas vendors will have 15 percent of the market nationwide.

A market share of 15 percent is enough to put pricing pressure on other retailers, so even if you don't buy gas at Costco or Wal-Mart, you'll pay less. A chain of gas stations appropriately named Clark Retail Enterprises Inc. filed for Chapter 11 bankruptcy protection in October 2002, blaming reduced profits due to price competition from Costco and Wal-Mart, according to a report in the *Chicago Tribune.* "The public will buy water for $2 or a Slim Jim for $1.69, but if the gasoline price is 4 cents more than at Wal-Mart, they take it personally," company president and CEO Brandon K. Barnholt told the newspaper.

Another way to tell that non-traditional gasoline retailers are having an impact is by the lawsuits and legislative attention they've attracted. In Florida, a number of lawsuits were filed claiming these retailers were violating a state law that bans deep discounting of gasoline. Wal-Mart, Sam's Club (which is owned by Wal-Mart), and Hess, an oil company, also faced lawsuits over gasoline discounting. The traditional oil companies and their dealers are trying to get laws passed in state legislature after state legislature outlawing discount gasoline. That's all because non-traditional vendors are winning a larger share of the market.

You'll save about 15 cents a gallon buying gas from a discounter versus a branded location and about five cents a gallon compared to a low-priced independent station. You can buy with even more confidence from a seller that guarantees its gas, as some discounters do, than a brand-name seller that won't. I've never heard a complaint from someone who bought gas from a discounter and had a problem.

I once visited a "tanker farm" for a major gasoline brand, and I was astounded to see tanker trucks from many different companies filling up at the same place. I had always believed each gas had a special secret formula, but a relative who worked there told me that all the companies give each other gas. The oil companies dispute this, but there's never been any independent verification that there are any significant differences in different brands of gas.

Another way to save money on gasoline is to buy regular gas, not the more expensive premium grades. Only 5 percent of all cars actually need premium gas, yet 20 percent of all gas sold is premium. So a lot of people are paying more for premium who don't need to do so. Thanks to advertising, people believe that buying premium is better for their cars, but the truth is you could cause long-term damage to the engine by buying a higher grade than you need. Look in your owner's manual to see what kind of gas your car requires.

The cost of buying more-expensive gas can add up. Premium costs 20 cents more a gallon. For a 15-gallon fill-up, that's $3 more every time you fill up, as much as $300 a year.

• Tips on Gasoline •

○ You'll save about 5 to 15 cents a gallon buying gas from a discounter, and the gas is just as good as gas from a brand-name station.

○ Don't buy premium gas unless your owner's manual says you need premium.

BARGAINS + INFORMATION ONLINE

(Clark's home page: www.clarkhoward.com)

FOOD

www.consumerreports.org	(Tests of water filters)
www.couponmountain.com	(Grocery coupons)
www.cutouthunger.org	(Grocery coupons)
www.entertainment.com	(Entertainment coupon book)
www.epicurious.com	(Information about wine)
www.intowine.com	(Information about wine)
www.oregonwine.org	(Information about wine, focusing on Oregon wine)
www.salesmountain.com	(Grocery coupons)
www.wineloverspage.com	(Information about wine)
www.zagat.com	(Restaurant survey)

FAMILY & CHILDREN

www.about-dogs.com	(Dog breeds and characteristics)
www.fda.gov	(Information about baby formula)
www.hsus.org	(The Humane Society of the United States)
www.parentware.org	(Financial software for children)
www.petcarerx.com	(Discount online pet pharmacy)
www.safekids.org	(Safety tips for children's products)

NECESSITIES

www.canadameds.com	(Discount prescription drugs from Canada)
www.lensexpress.com	(Discount contact lenses)
www.rxaminer.com	(Cheaper alternatives to prescribed drugs)

LEISURE

www.amazon.com	(Savings on books)
www.bamm.com	(Savings on books)
www.cdnow.com	(Buy and download music)
www.entertainment.com	(Entertainment coupon book)
www.half.com	(Used items at discount prices)
www.emusic.com	(Buy and download music)
www.halfpricebooks.com	(Savings on books)
www.mtv.com	(Buy and download music)
www.netflix.com	(DVD rentals)
www.ouraaa.com	(Discount movie tickets from AAA)

ELECTRONICS & APPLIANCES

www.consumerreports.org	(Reliability reports on appliances)
www.energystar.gov	(Energy efficiency information)

EVENTS

www.evite.com	(Online invitations)
www.funerals.org	(Information about burial and cremation)
www.theknot.com	(Wedding planning)

HOME IMPROVEMENT

www.carpetsofdalton.com	(Carpets of Dalton)
www.cfi-installers.org	(Carpet and flooring installers)
www.ikea.com	(IKEA)
www.galleryfurniture.com	(Gallery Furniture)
www.nebraskafurnituremart.com	(Nebraska Furniture Mart)
www.nofma.org	(The Wood Flooring Manufacturers Association)
www.overstock.com	(Online liquidator)
www.southface.org	(Southface Energy Institute)
www.smartbargains.com	(Bargains on housewares)
www.tuesdaymorning.com	(Bargains on housewares)
www.valuecity.com	(Bargains on housewares)
www.woodfloors.org	(To buy wood flooring)

CARS

www.aaa.com	(Automobile Club of America)
www.consumerreports.org	(Tire quality report)
www.costco.com	(Emergency Road Service plan)
www.mapquest.com	(Driving directions)
www.samsclub.com	(Emergency Road Service plan)
www.tirerack.com	(Buying tires online)

Also available from Clark Howard, America's favorite radio show host.

"It could be worth a fortune."

– USA Today

This *Wall Street Journal* business bestseller shows you how to:

- Get the best airfares, hotel rates, and car rentals – sometimes 90% below advertised rates.
- Invest for retirement now, without feeling the pinch.
- Prevent identity theft – and save hours of headaches and legal bills.
- Deal with a health club when you want to leave.
- Negotiate like a pro when buying a home.
- Buy a great car and never get stuck with a lemon.

0-7868-8777-X
Paperback

ClarkHoward.com

How much money can Clark Howard save *you*?

Listen to "The Clark Howard Show" on your local radio station.